BUSINESS
COMMUNICATION
IN A TECHNOLOGICAL WORLD

Second Edition

Brandy Fair ‖ Chris Gurrie

Cover image © Shutterstock, Inc.

Kendall Hunt
publishing company

www.kendallhunt.com
Send all inquiries to:
4050 Westmark Drive
Dubuque, IA 52004-1840

Copyright © 2017, 2022 by Kendall Hunt Publishing Company

PAK ISBN 978-1-7924-2876-0
Text alone ISBN 979-8-7657-0077-8

Printed in the United States of America

Contents

"What if, and I know this sounds kooky, we communicated with the employees."

© Cartoon Resource/Shutterstock.com

So, how many of you are really excited about taking a business communication course? Our guess is a lot of you are required to take this class and it was not something you were looking forward to registering for this term. Either you A) decided to take this class right off the bat to get it over with, or B) you have waited until the very last semester before you are ready to graduate and have put this moment off until the end of your college career. Sound about right? Many of you are probably wondering, "Why do I have to take a business speech course, I talk every day? I don't have a problem; I know how to interact with people." It is not that you do not know how to communicate, but our goal is to provide tips and tricks to be *more effective* in how you communicate in your everyday life.

Year after year Fortune 500 groups, HR directors, CEOs, etc. express how important communication is within their workplaces. Unfortunately, a college degree alone is not enough anymore. You have to strive to be above and beyond just completing coursework. Earning a degree with a 4.0 GPA is great, but you also need to show diversity in your abilities with work and school. Good grades are important, but what other responsibilities did you juggle while earning your degree? Consider (if it is not too late in your college career) joining clubs and organizations on campus, holding officer positions within those groups, include your work experience while you were taking courses, etc. Show potential employers that you are a well-rounded individual, who can handle multiple responsibilities. Build that resume up!

The chart below shows the top 15 skills employers identified as important and key factors in determining who they hire into their organization. The list is broken down into top technical skills, top soft skills, and top qualities that make an individual more hireable. Many of the technical skills grew in importance as we found new ways to work, go to school, etc. during the pandemic. The soft skills and top qualities are probably not that surprising to see included; however, communication (both verbal and written) frequently appears on skills and qualities lists time and time again. Employers need to know they can turn to you and trust you can perform in stressful situations. That is why this communication course is so important in a business and professional environment – in our technological world. Our job is to help you do your job even better.

The Top 15 Skills and Qualities Employers are Looking For

Top Technical Skills	Top Soft Skills	Top Qualities that Make You more Hirable
1. Cloud computing	6. Communication	11. Honesty
2. Data presentation	7. Problem-Solving	12. Loyalty
3. Search Engine Optimization (SEO)	8. Time Management	13. Determination
4. Mobile Development	9. Organization	14. Personal Work Ethic
5. Network Security	10. Collaborative Skills	15. Eagerness to Learn & Adapt

Source: ZipJob Team. (2022). *Top 15 Skills Employers Are Hiring For in 2022*. https://www.zipjob.com/blog/skills-employers-are-looking-for/

Starting off, we need some basic foundational information. Let us begin with a basic definition of what communication actually is. **Communication** is a systemic process in which people interact with and through symbols to create and interpret meanings. I know the definition seems wordy, so we will break this definition down so it actually makes sense. When you think communication, most people immediately go to the spoken language which is a symbol, but not the only option when communicating. How often do we communicate with somebody without saying a word? Our guess is your mom was excellent at giving you "the look" when you were in trouble. What messages can we communicate through body language?

Another part of that definition is that communication is a process. Communication is difficult and takes both sides being able to first, clearly communicate their message and second, clearly receive the message without interruptions and distractions. Easy enough right? Throughout the text, we will further examine the multitude of distractions that get in the way of good communication, both with the speaker and the audience.

Finally, communication is systemic; it is a system with certain parts needed in order for communication to take place. We will examine a communication model and discuss those elements needed in our process. First, you have to have at least one person sending a message so you have a **Sender** who delivers a **Message** to a **Receiver**. The message could be in a variety of forms: speech, memo, email, videoconference, etc.

"My last comment 'appeared' to be inviting feedback. Do not be fooled."

© Cartoon Resource/Shutterstock.com

The receiver could be a single person, a group of people, etc.; it is the person(s) who takes in that message. The receiver then provides **feedback** (some sort of acknowledgment the message was received) to the sender (Later on we will look at early models of communication and how feedback was not always part of the equation.). We all know communication does not happen that smoothly, and we face different obstacles for sending and receiving messages clearly; this is defined as noise. There are two types of noise – Internal Noise and External Noise. Most people are familiar with **External Noise**, those outside distractions that get in the way of us sending or receiving a message. This could be the person sitting next to you tapping their pen, coughs/sneezes, traffic around you, etc. The other type of noise is **Internal Noise**, those voices and thoughts in your head that distract from sending or receiving a message. Yes, you have voices in your head! How many times do we get distracted by stress, our "to do" list of errands for the day, thinking about a relationship, etc.? Those competing thoughts make it difficult to effectively send or receive new information.

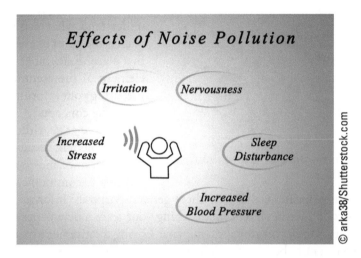

The last element to talk about with the communication model is the Field of Experience. You will see that one circle represents the Sender, and there is also a circle that represents the Receiver. Each circle represents the knowledge base for that person/group. For example, the Sender has information they are familiar with, topics they can discuss, etc. as does the Receiver. Where the two circles overlap is called the **Field of Experience** - what the sender and the receiver have in common. This element becomes extremely important when considering topic selection for presentations. What does your audience know about the topic already? When the audience is already familiar with the subject, then you can start with more advanced material. However, if it is brand new information for the audience, you have got to break it down to make sure that everybody understands what you are discussing. Sometimes, the only thing you and your audience will have in common is you are in the same place at the same time, so you have to consider that when going through the topic-selection process. We will cover topic selection in more depth in a future chapter.

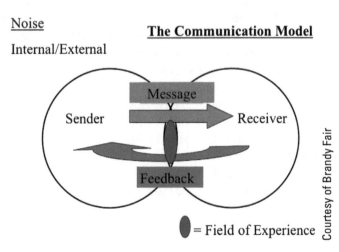

"Everything on your resume is true ... right?"

Understanding the basic elements is the first step, but there are other items to consider when crafting your own message whether it is one-on-one conversation or giving a presentation to 1,000 people. Remember that your *message needs to be understood.* If the audience does not understand what you are talking about then what is the point of even communicating in the first place? Remember that field-of-experience element of the communication model when preparing your information. Will the audience grasp the concepts?

Have a goal. Although we all know those people who talk because they like the sound of their own voice, most of us have a purpose when it comes to communicating with others. When it comes to business communication, there are three general purposes: inform, persuade, and entertain (or a combination of any of the three). Are you teaching your team a new paperwork process? Trying to convince potential investors to buy from your company? Giving a retirement speech for a colleague? No matter the situation, you want to be sure that you are achieving your goals.

Be honest and ethical. Do not lie to your audience! We have seen countless examples in the business world of people getting caught lying on their resumes and getting caught.

https://www.marketwatch.com/story/5-big-shots-who-lied-on-their-resumes-2014-09-18.

It is important to be honest to your audience no matter what. Even if you do not know the answer, the solution is not to make one up. It is perfectly acceptable to say, "I don't know, that's a great question. Let me find the answer for you." Yes, you want to prepare for possible questions that may arise, but unfortunately we cannot prepare for everything. It is your job as a presenter to find the answer and provide the correct information when appropriate.

Do not forget to *Consider Your Audience.* Despite completing your research, having a clear goal, and practicing your delivery over and over, your speech could fall on deaf ears if your audience has no idea what you are talking about. Be sure to go through the process of audience analysis, or what can you determine about your audience before you ever take the stage. Are they a group of your peers? Presenting to your bosses? Talking about a new idea to potential clients? Realize that you could present the same speech topic in hundreds of different ways based on who receives the message. You may have to ask questions of the individuals who asked you to speak to find out whom your audience is if you are starting from square one. If possible, you could also send out a survey to who will be attending to find out if they are already familiar with your topic or what they hope to learn/gain from your session so you can prepare your presentation accordingly. The worst feeling is to work diligently on a speech to find out the audience already has that information.

Check Your Space. At the start of a professional development session, a guest speaker was having difficulty with the wireless microphone. He kept trying to adjust it, but the back half of the room could not hear him at all. His initial response was to just go ahead with the presentation. The audience immediately protested, as they could not make out what he was saying. The individual who booked the session ran to get a handheld microphone to switch out. Although the new microphone was loud enough, it had terrible high-pitched feedback for the entire presentation. How much do you think the audience gained from being at the session?

The lesson – check your space. No matter what type of speaking engagement situation, always check the space and equipment beforehand. What is the room design? How will the audience be seated (and can you adjust, if needed)? Does the technology work (PowerPoint, microphone, videos, etc.)? The one thing to keep in mind is **Murphy's Law** – "if something can go wrong, it will go wrong." What does that mean for you as a presenter? Always have a backup plan! You want to be prepared for any situation that may arise. If the projector does not work, have handouts ready just in case. If video clips will not play, have scenarios ready to discuss and work through with the audience. Whatever you have planned, always have a Plan B ready to go. If you have a backup, you probably would not need it. It is when presenters are *not* ready for the "what if" that things often go south.

Although these are just a few key elements to start off with, they build the foundation for any type of presentation you will face. No matter what speaking scenario you encounter, they are essential items to consider. Keep in mind the potential for mishaps to occur, which leads to another key point when it comes to business communication – *Be Adaptable.* Trust us, we wish we could teach you the magic "one way" to communicate and it would never fail. Unfortunately, what works with one situation does not always translate to the next. Have you ever heard the saying "You can't step in the same river twice?" The lesson is that the river is constantly changing, as does each situation where you will need to speak. Adaptability allows for new prospects in the business environment. Here are a few reasons why adaptability in the workplace can work in your favor.

1. You will be a "go to" person at work. If your supervisor knows you can handle any kind of curve ball headed your way, then they will trust you with more and more responsibilities.
2. New opportunities can come your way. One of the best pieces of advice I received when starting a new position was to say "yes" to anything asked of you within the first year. "Can you do some research on this for me? Will you stay late to work on this project? Will you head a committee?" etc. Although this seems like you have to take on extra work (and you do), it gives you the opportunity to prove yourself to higher-ups in the organization. People start learning who you are, know you by name, and know you complete good work. Granted there comes a time where you will need to start saying no so you do not take on too much, but being a "no" person right up front does not open up doors to new possibilities.
3. Realize everyone communicates differently. We will discuss this further as we dive into information regarding culture and demographics, but understand you might have to deliver the same information in multiple ways to make sure everyone receives the message. This is a concept every good teacher practices. It would be great to present information one way and know every student understood the concepts; however, that perfect scenario is rare. Try to think of other examples, scenarios, or ways to explain the concept, if someone is confused. Remember to stay patient and do your best to adapt your audience's needs.

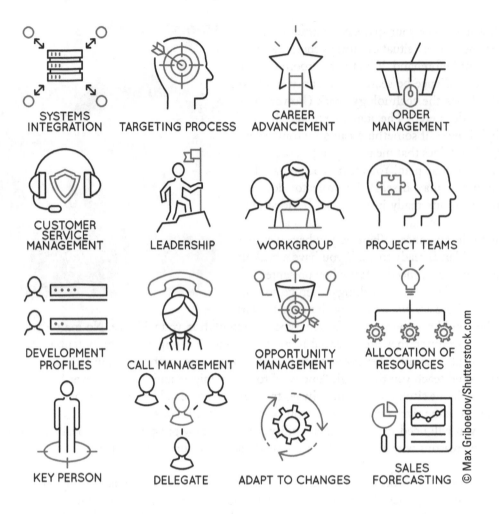

© Max Griboedov/Shutterstock.com

Communication Apprehension

We opened the chapter asking how many of you dreaded taking this class; our guess is one response includes, "I am afraid of public speaking." Guess what? – You are not alone. In research, the term glossophobia or "speech anxiety" may often appear.

In the communication field, this is referred to as **communication apprehension**. What is important to know about communication apprehension is that it is not just public speaking; instead, it refers to a person's level of anxiety associated with either real or anticipated communication with another person or persons. Yes, public speaking falls into this definition, but it can

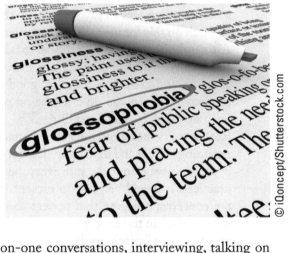

© iQoncept/Shutterstock.com

include all types of communication: small groups, one-on-one conversations, interviewing, talking on the phone, etc. Richard McCroskey was one of the founding researchers in communication apprehension and broke it down into two different categories: trait and state apprehension.

When talking about **trait apprehension**, focus on the word "trait." Often people think of different human traits: outgoing, eye color, interests, etc. A person with trait apprehension is fearful of all forms of communication. It is not that they cannot or would not communicate, but they are not going to be the first to volunteer to give a presentation. These individuals often may be described as shy or introverted. **State apprehension** occurs because of different factors in communication that raises their anxiety. There may be a certain type or "context" of communication that makes them nervous; for a lot of people, it is the public speaking setting. Jerry Seinfeld has a joke that the number one fear in America is public speaking; number two – death. So, at a funeral, more people would rather be in the casket than giving the eulogy. Beyond the context, maybe the "audience" makes the speaker nervous. Perhaps you are fine giving a speech in front of your peers in the communication classroom; what happens if you have to give the same speech in front of your bosses, the CEO, or HR director? Finally, the entire "situation" can impact state apprehension. It is a combination of unique factors that occurs that maybe you have never faced before. You have done public speaking events, you organize meetings in your business, but now you have to run a meeting for 100 strangers to sell a product. Maybe you have to give a toast at a wedding. The situation is new and may cause higher anxiety.

Below is a copy of the Personal Report of Communication Apprehension (PRCA). It is a short survey to have a basic understanding of your level of communication apprehension.

Personal Report of Communication Apprehension (PRCA-24)

Directions: This instrument is composed of 24 statements concerning feelings about communicating with others. Please indicate the degree to which each statement applies to you by marking whether you:

Strongly Disagree = 1; Disagree = 2; are Neutral = 3; Agree = 4; Strongly Agree = 5

_____ 1. I dislike participating in group discussions.

_____ 2. Generally, I am comfortable while participating in group discussions.

_____ 3. I am tense and nervous while participating in group discussions.

_____ 4. I like to get involved in group discussions.

_____ 5. Engaging in a group discussion with new people makes me tense and nervous.

_____ 6. I am calm and relaxed while participating in group discussions.

_____ 7. Generally, I am nervous when I have to participate in a meeting.

_____ 8. Usually, I am comfortable when I have to participate in a meeting.

_____ 9. I am very calm and relaxed when I am called upon to express an opinion at a meeting.

_____10. I am afraid to express myself at meetings.

_____11. Communicating at meetings usually makes me uncomfortable.

_____12. I am very relaxed when answering questions at a meeting.

_____13. While participating in a conversation with a new acquaintance, I feel very nervous.

_____14. I have no fear of speaking up in conversations.

_____15. Ordinarily I am very tense and nervous in conversations.

_____16. Ordinarily I am very calm and relaxed in conversations.

_____17. While conversing with a new acquaintance, I feel very relaxed.

_____18. I'm afraid to speak up in conversations.

_____19. I have no fear of giving a speech.

_____20. Certain parts of my body feel very tense and rigid while giving a speech.

_____21. I feel relaxed while giving a speech.

_____22. My thoughts become confused and jumbled when I am giving a speech.

_____23. I face the prospect of giving a speech with confi dence.

_____24. While giving a speech, I get so nervous I forget facts I really know.

SCORING:

Group discussion: 18 - (scores for items 2, 4, & 6) + (scores for items 1, 3, & 5)

Meetings: 18 - (scores for items 8, 9, & 12) + (scores for items 7, 10, & 11)

Interpersonal: 18 - (scores for items 14, 16, & 17) + (scores for items 13, 15, & 18)

Public Speaking: 18 - (scores for items 19, 21, & 23) + (scores for items 20, 22, & 24)

Group Discussion Score: _____

Interpersonal Score: _____

Meetings Score: _____

Public Speaking Score: _____

To obtain your total score for the PRCA, simply add your sub-scores together. _____

Scores can range from 24–120. Scores below 51 represent people who have very low CA. Scores between 51–80 represent people with average CA. Scores above 80 represent people who have high levels of trait CA.

NORMS FOR THE PRCA-24: (based on over 40,000 college students; data from over 3,000 non-student adults in a national sample provided virtually identical norms, within 0.20 for all scores.)

Mean	Standard Deviation	High	Low
Total Score: 65.6	15.3	> 80	< 51
Group: 15.4	4.8	> 20	< 11
Meeting: 16.4	4.2	> 20	< 13
Dyad (Interpersonal): 14.2	3.9	> 18	< 11
Public: 19.3	5.1	> 24	< 14

No matter what level of apprehension you experience, trust us, we all deal with nerves (even those of us in the communication field)! It is about how you handle the apprehension that will determine your success. Here are a few tips to keep in mind to help handle our anxiety.

1. Recognize the source of your anxiety and learn how to fight it. What makes you nervous? If it is the situation, then you need to put yourself in that situation more often and not avoid it. I know several people who are nervous about interviewing and would hate to lose that dream job because of anxiety. So to fight it, they would interview for jobs they did not necessarily want just to practice different interview questions and being in the hot seat. If public speaking is your fear, then find avenues to speak in front of people such as groups at work or organizations such as Toastmasters.

2. Know your strengths and weaknesses. We usually have a pretty decent idea of what we are good at and where we could improve. You do not want to practice and focus only on what you do well! If you are not the best at moving around the room while speaking, then work more on scripting movement and how/when it will occur. Build up on your weaknesses, so you are not overly stressed about them while speaking. If you focus on mistakes

© kenary820/Shutterstock.com

© BlueSkyImage/Shutterstock.com

From *An Introduction to Rhetorical Communication: A Western Rhetorical Perspective*, 9/e by James C. McCroskey. Copyright © 2015 Taylor & Francis Group LLC-Books. Reprinted by permission.

without working to improve them, the odds of continuing to make the same errors increase like a self-fulfilling prophecy. You expected to mess up and so you do.

3. Know how you react to stress. Are you a fast talker? Do you shake? Start to sweat? If you prepare for the effects, then they will not damage your presentation as much. For the three examples above, think about scheduling time to breathe in the speech if you speak quickly (some people forget!), avoid holding items in your hands if you shake, and wear dark clothing, so sweat is less noticeable. Minimize the impact.

© Sarawut Aiemsinsuk/Shutterstock.com

In addition, NEVER tell the audience you are nervous, you are not prepared, this will be terrible, etc. Do not give the audience any reason not to listen to you right up front! You are more nervous than the audience realizes, unless you tell them!

4. Practice in front of a group and test your message. The first word is key – Practice!

That does not mean moments before you speak either. It is amazing to see speakers prepare their notes moments before they hit the stage instead of preparing them ahead of time to practice going through them during the speech. The more you review your information, the greater the retention, and the better the presentation. Testing your message means that it will make sense to your audience. Is the content clear? Jokes are funny? "Abuse" your friends, family, colleagues and have them sit through or read through your presentation for clarity. If they are lost or confused, odds are your audience will have a similar reaction.

5. Visualize success. When you practice, go through the entire presentation as if it is the real moment. Avoid stopping and restarting, pausing to take care of others tasks, etc. because that will not happen during the actual speech. Remember, each time you go through the content (even if you make mistakes), you will improve with each run-through and start eliminating the nervous errors. If you can do a run-through in the actual space, it is great so you know your environment. Familiarity with the room setup, technology you will use, and how you actually sound in the space will help calm nerves too.

6. Relaxation and breathing strategies. We highly recommend breathing in a presentation!

Nerves can cause us to speed up and forget to take that all important breath!

© Poniz/Shutterstock.com

It is ok to take a second (even several!) throughout your presentation to collect your thoughts and breathe. It may feel like forever to you, but the audience will not notice anything. If you find you speed up or struggle to breathe during a speech, it might be a good idea to actually give cues to yourself in your notes to take a breath at different points in the presentation.

7. Concentrate on the message. Focus on what you have prepared, the examples you want to give, the sources you will present, etc. Yes, you want to pay attention to your audience, but your first job is to deliver a solid presentation. You have worked hard to prepare for the moment, so you want to put your best foot forward with your own delivery.

Overall, this introductory chapter introduces us to the difficult process of communication. We examined the basic elements of communication, some important ideas to consider when preparing a message, and how each of us may fight with communication apprehension. Just because it is not a formal speech does not mean we can ignore the basics of communicating. Each message should have a clear purpose, attend to the audience, and we must be ready to adapt to the reactions we receive no matter if it is a business meeting, conference call, or sales pitch. Welcome to *Business Communication in a Technological World*.

Chapter

2 Culture

© Rawpixel.com/Shutterstock.com

Students of higher education come from all walks of life: socioeconomic status, race, religion, gender, sexuality, etc. These characteristics are known as demographics. However, we will not use this chapter to highlight demographics that often spend more time underscoring our differences rather than our similarities. Instead, we will explore the culture of business and the professions. This culture, the culture of business, is where those demographics come into play.

To some, "business" is working in a cube at a computer for 8 hours a day. For others, their business may be the military—and the military is a well-oiled organization. For others still, farms, families, and churches are also long-understood organizations, some of which are run like businesses. For the basis of this text, what we must understand is that the "culture" of business is not synonymous with "Corporate America." Sports, medicine, technological applications like Uber and Airbnb, and an online T-shirt business are all organizations where communication is key and technology imperative.

Corporate Culture

The United States has created an environment (for better or worse) that has allowed people with dreams of business ownership to grow those dreams into large corporate operations. America has given birth to Starbucks, Google, AT&T, American Airlines, Walmart, Ernst & Young, and many other household businesses. Each of these named companies has its own internal culture—the way people are treated, behaviors, the way people dress, what is valued, the management style, etc. With more workers using telecommuting than ever before, some cultures have been upended, some left alone, and others waiting to see what happens in the next few years. However, one thing many Americans can agree on is that there is a distinct feeling to "corporate culture."

Corporate culture usually yields thoughts and feelings that are more formal. An employee adheres to standards of professionalism that include more formal dress, more formal writing and speaking, certain rules and rituals of when to arrive, how to address clients, and when vacation time can be requested and taken to name a few. Corporate culture typically includes a "place of business" such as an office building or campus where an employee spends his or her days working in their selected fields.

Born out of the manufacturing world of the previous centuries, large corporate cultures are traditionally very regimented. Companies strive for uniformity in products and services that span across state and

© Everett Historical/Shutterstock.com

country boundaries. Anywhere in the world one goes, they can expect a certain product or level of service from a certain company. This is how large businesses build a brand. As such, employees adhere to a set of standards that help maintain that brand.

To some of the creative types, this may be too "stuffy" for their free-thinking minds. For others, this is exactly the type of company and environment where they will thrive—working for a large company and using their talents to assist in a greater brand. As the world progresses, Millennials have influenced workforces, and as the way business is conducted continues to change, so too does corporate culture. We will call this "**creative culture**."

Creative Culture

When you study organizations, business books, popular podcasts, or the "hottest places to work," you will most definitely come across Google. An American corporate success story, Google was one of the premiere companies to gain notoriety for changing the corporate culture. Google introduced flexible work schedules, increased the idea of "fun" in the workplace in order to nurture creative thinking, and offered different perks like an on-campus gym and restaurant to attract top talent—and keep it.

Other companies took notice and, slowly but steadily, organizations have started to offer various perks and opportunities different from the traditional corporate culture. One of the most prevalent of these changes is flexible schedules and telecommuting. More companies and organizations are offering employees the opportunity to create their own schedules so long as the necessary work is completed.

Others create organizations based on telecommuting where an employee may work remotely some or all of the time they work for the company. Then 2020 happened.

Telecommuting was something discussed as a "perk" to some businesses, or a necessity or necessity for various industries where face-to-face meeting was quite difficult. Many forward-thinking universities offered online courses including their MBA and nursing programs, just as rigorous, but the delivery methods were different. At times, the traditional culture of thought may not have found these methods as sound as "the old ways." However, once 2020 and the pandemic struck business, telecommuting (now called virtual (for virtually everything)) was a necessity for businesses to remain afloat. Below we mention how this telecommuting began, readers over the age of 10 know how it continued. In some cases the culture improved (telehealth, meetings with advisors, etc.) and in some cases many were ready to get back to in-person work (yoga, gym training, concerts, conferences).

The great recession of 2008 increased the speed of implementation of online and telecommuting practices because it is lower in overhead and costs less to keep smaller physical spaces. Other organizations recognized large high-rise office space and mall locations as cost ineffective, so they reduced staff and/or allowed more staff to work remotely. Today, we have entire companies that exist without physical space for most of their "employees." Think: Uber, Airbnb, much of Amazon, StubHub, and more.

The purpose of mentioning creative culture here is for students of business communication to be aware of the ever-changing nature of organizations, which alters and amends the way people within the organization communicate. When working within a creative culture, you may spend much of your time writing and editing in a certain software; perhaps, you may be on the phone most of the day and write very little. Back when corporate culture was growing, you had to make a conscious effort to get to know a colleague at work. It is important to be aware of how creative cultures write, read, listen, interact, use social media, interview, and train. Knowing your audience and colleagues will allow you to adapt your communication strategy accordingly.

The inability to adapt communication strategy to the specific organizational culture can sometimes result in friction between people. We discussed this briefly in chapter one when we discussed the communication model. Understanding the sender and receiver frames of experience is so important. Consider for a moment the Baby Boomer-aged manager, who does not understand why her younger employees Tweet and text their clients; going so far as to call it "too casual" or disrespectful. However, those employees are aware of their audience—their Generation X clients—and are using a method of communication to address them in a way they have requested. So, in the end, the employees are being extremely effective by using a convenient means of communication once thought too casual. We will examine these different groups further in another chapter.

The Culture of Closeness

What a time to be alive! You may have a very active (or dusty) Facebook page, work on LinkedIn, solid Twitter account, and possibly an Instagram, Snapchat, and TikTok. All of these platforms allow users to customize and personalize their online space. Never before have so many media allowed the general public to be so visible and accessible. With this innovation comes some caution. The caution of divulging too much about yourself, or possibly worse, finding out things about your colleagues you never wanted to know.

Back when corporate culture was growing, to get to know a colleague at work you had to really try. Perhaps your coworker had pictures of his wife on his desk, or always wore red and blue tie colors to represent his college. It took questions and nuance to get to know people and their interests, hobbies, and habits. You may have known someone had kids, but it took a lot of discussion to learn more about them.

Then came social media. Now, if you connect with someone on social media, getting to "know" them can take no time at all. And, there are possible dangers with this. On one person's Instagram story, there may be posts about politics, religion, social issues, and controversy. Typically, not topics openly discussed in the workplace, these concepts could quickly become wedge issues between colleagues. The bottom line: be careful as you navigate this new culture of closeness. Maybe only allow people onto your social media that you would allow into your home. Perhaps create only one profile you allow work people to access. There are several ways to clean up your "media brand," but now more than ever it is necessary to be aware of how you are perceived and how others perceive you.

Workplace Diversity

We would be remiss if we did not mention the increased diversity of the American workforce and the United States as a nation. According to the Economics Policy Institute, by 2032 the working majority of the US will be comprised of minority populations. Always a nation of immigrants, the domestic workforce continues to change as attitudes toward work and who does it continue to progress.

Consider not that long ago women attended college to be nurses or teachers. There were few female doctors, police officers, or engineers. Today, many college female populations outnumber males; and disciplines like business, the sciences, and law see women entering

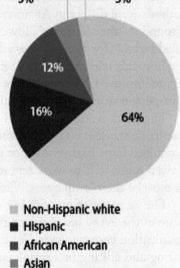

People of color make up nearly one-third of the labor force

- Non-Hispanic white
- Hispanic
- African American
- Asian
- Did not identify racially or ethnically

Source: Bureau of Labor Statistics.

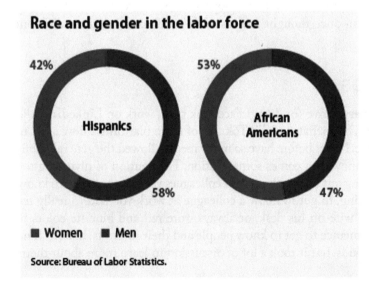

Race and gender in the labor force

Hispanics — Women 42%, Men 58%
African Americans — Women 53%, Men 47%

- Women ■ Men

Source: Bureau of Labor Statistics.

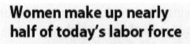

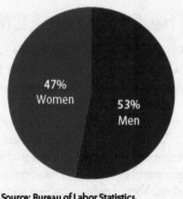

Women make up nearly half of today's labor force

47% Women
53% Men

Source: Bureau of Labor Statistics.

in record numbers each year. People of color from all heritages and backgrounds are joining the US workforce out of necessity, breaking culture molds and norms, and the changing model of US families.

Taboos around men staying at home with families, working from home, or not working at all have changed. Masculine pride once assigned to earning cash in corporate culture has begun to shift to taking pride in one's family, one's home, or one's small business. As such, we see more men today with flexible schedules and parental duties than we did just 50 years ago.

Organizational culture, especially in larger towns and cities, will bring more diverse people together working toward a common goal. Race, class, sexual orientation, gender identity, religion, and other demographics will help shape the cultures of organizations. Studies show that diverse workforces enrich companies and increase revenue and enjoyment. As more college grads pour into the job market, it is essential to be aware of diversity, embrace it, and use communication practices that promote understanding and teamwork.

Understanding Your Audience

Speech class 101 rule #1 of speech-making: **know your audience**. Most likely your instructor has discussed this with you, or soon will. There is a lot of power in this little rule – a rule that can be applied to just about every context. Want to catch your criminal, you have *know* your criminal. Want to sell BMWs to your client, you have to *know* your client. Want to run a successful business, you have to *know* your customers. Large multinational companies have learned this the hard way over the years. About 15 years ago, Walmart discovered its formula of low prices and large box stores is not a one-size-fits-all recipe for success. The retailer was unsuccessful in Germany because it did not understand the local culture and shopping habits of the Germans. This story reported in the New York Times (Landler & Barbaro, 2006) is widely discussed in business schools for its perfect case study value of helping students and business people understand the utter importance of knowing one's audience. The same article reports that Walmart struggled in Asian cultures as well for not understanding the shopping behavior of the customers as well as their loyalty to local chains.

© Rob Crandall/Shutterstock.com

McDonald's is a corporation that strives to understand the local cultures in which it operates. If you have traveled outside of North America and visited a McDonald's, then you have seen this. In Paris, you will find baguettes on the menu. In the Middle East, you may find meats prepared Halal according to religious practices; in Japan, you may indulge in the Tsukimi burger, and, in India, you can try a Big Mac prepared with a chicken patty to honor the culture of not eating beef. McDonald's teams have worked hard to understand the habits and culture of local populations in order to create products to drive the most business.

Also, in speech class 101, new speakers learning about their audiences are taught that one of the best ways to find information about the said audience is to *ask*. We mention this because the same rule may apply when learning about cultures different from your own. Often, the best way to learn about that culture is to simply ask. Sometimes, the literature in books and on the Internet is overly stereotyped or generalized in a way that could be detrimental to your doing business in that culture. For example, when learning about doing business in Arab countries, one may read in books much about Islamic culture and how Muslims do not drink alcohol or engage in some other typically Western customs. Upon arrival to certain countries, you may be startled to find bars and restaurants that serve alcohol. Of course, this is because those countries *know* their Western audience and have created establishments to help drive business and make their colleagues feel welcome. While Muslims themselves may not partake in alcoholic beverages, this example highlights something one may learn about only by asking members of that city or country; or by asking the great Google machine specifically.

Understanding the culture of your "audience" is just as important when doing business closer to home. We need not always think of international examples to highlight the importance of understanding organizational culture. The United States has many examples of its own that highlight the necessity for awareness when communicating with others outside your cultural domain. Elements of region, religion, immigration, and education affect local American cultures across the states. As a Northeasterner, you may be surprised to find a business meeting in the South opened with a prayer. Southerners may be shocked to see the "beer culture" of Wisconsin is more than an old stereotype, and if you plan on doing business in Miami, you best brush up on your Spanish, as Spanish is widely spoken there and in California.

The purpose in discussing these **cultural characteristics** is for you, the student of business communication, to think of ways to engage members of your organization in communication from a creative perspective that embraces diverse colleagues of all walks of life. Diversity and culture can help strengthen ideas and bring new perspectives to an organization. Harnessing this power can help grow an organization and make it more successful. Moreover, technology continues to bring the world closer together.

Some tips for preparing to engage with different cultures:

1. Research. Whether it is people working with you in your local Texan company, Millennials in your workplace, or international students in your college work group, researching cultural demographics can help you better understand your colleagues.
2. Ask. If you are honestly seeking information about a culture, asking professional and honest questions can help you better understand those with whom you are working. You may ask members of that culture directly or those you know personally who may be part of that culture.
3. Seek to understand for prosperity. Remember not to criticize other cultures for doing something "weird." Instead, realize that things are done differently. Seeking to understand these differences will make you seem professional and intellectual.

Choosing to ignore cultural characteristics from different parts of the country or world is no longer an option. Ignorance to diversity may result in obsolescence to the fault of your business or organization.

© Rawpixel.com/Shutterstock.com

We hope that learning to communicate with different people will help grow your business and enrich the work you do.

The main focus of this chapter on culture is to highlight that *culture* means many things. We set out to discuss more traditional corporate culture and moved to creative culture with the purpose of embracing many different types of workplaces – especially when discussing *business communication* in a technological world. The purpose in doing so is for you, the student, to consider how you would approach your communication strategy based on the context and type of culture in which you are working. Being aware of how others around you communicate will allow you to select the appropriate tools to be best understood. Ultimately, communication is for understanding, and understanding leads to sales, promotions, closed deals, and revenue.

Since the publication of this text in 2017 the US and parts of the world have seen increased attention paid to diversity, equity, and inclusion in all facets of life. Within the American fabric we've witnessed the cultural events of George Floyd, Breonna Taylor, and Ahmaud Arbery. We've mourned school shootings of and by young people (and others) where violence spoke for deeper rooted problems of isolation, racism, nationalism, radicalism, and beyond. As social media becomes simply "media," we've seen more and more average citizens post their political, racial, and ethical views online–resulting in increased visibility sometimes fraught with negative consequences. Conversely, marginalized groups within racial, ethnic, social, and other lanes have found meeting space to avoid feeling alone. We've heard conversations about toxic masculinity, White privilege, and cancel culture. We've seen athletes further turned into celebrities by way of social media, and we've seen celebrities turned into Presidents by the same avenue. We've seen unknown people become rich overnight with clever moves against the market and we've seen a crazy housing market price out many Millennials in their 30s. We know most people under 40 couldn't stand to watch a "TV schedule" set by the traditional networks or have time or access to the local television news. Finally, we can guess you're still talking or hearing about Bitcoin yet are unsure what it does or have yet to find more than one person to adequately explain it. We also hope you've avoided those essential oils and multi-level marketing schemes known as at-home businesses. We've seen new companies solve problems, private people in space, and a female vice president. All this is to say, the culture in America and around the globe is changing—and quickly. Knowing, understanding, and being dynamic will be the way to use communication to effectively move in a positive direction.

We conclude the chapter with a nod toward the ever-changing face of the American workforce, the United States, and the world. Understanding people have different backgrounds, but really are not all that different when working for a common goal will allow for a rich, vibrant, thoughtful work experience that could also lead to more sales, more deals closed, and better relationships. It is imperative to do research and select the communication tools right for the situations.

REFERENCE

Landler, M., & Barbaro, M. (2006). Wal-Mart Finds that It's Formula Doesn't Fit Every Culture. *The New York Times*.

Chapter
3 Perception of Self and Others

© Prajak Poonyawatpornkul/Shutterstock.com

The first day of class is sometimes lovingly referred to as "seat day." On this day, students arrive and scope out the classroom in order to choose where they will sit for what may arguably be the rest of the semester. Some choose to be right up front so they can hear, see, or be recognized. Some file to the back to duck out for work and family obligations or possibly to be less noticeable to others. This little psychological experiment goes on sometimes the rest of the term. Ever arrive and find someone "sitting in your seat?" The nerve! What is happening here are a series of quick judgments in order to create the space in which you want to learn. It may not be true for everyone, but many students know where they want to sit and why.

What some do not know is that for the professor a similar scene is unfolding. He/she is watching as students file into the classroom. The ones upfront—they are studious, honors students perhaps, or maybe the people who ask just too many questions. The ones in the back—taking the class as mandatory, possibly slackers or people who work and need to accept phone calls without disturbing the class. And, what about this student in the middle so well dressed? She must "mean business" or perhaps she has an internship?

The bottom-line here—perception. We make judgments based on cues, and we use these cues as sense-making techniques in order to better understand the world in which we operate. Sometimes right, sometimes wrong, perception lies with the receiver and many times we do not have the opportunity to correct a misperception.

We use "seat day" in the classroom as an example to highlight simple things that may or may not be correct. The woman up front may simply not want to be distracted by any of the open laptops around her. The guy in the back may not feel good and want to sit as close to the exit as possible. The people not dressed up are not lazy; they come from their yoga classes. The list can go on. The purpose of this chapter is to highlight the concept of self-perception and how others perceive us. When communicating in business and professional contexts, it is important to consider how messages created and sent will be decoded, understand the possible perceptions they will send, and work to achieve maximum communication impact. Thinking back to the communication model from chapter one, it is important to remember that message meanings can differ between the sender and receiver.

© ibreakstock/Shutterstock.com

Perception Process

A Google search will tell you that **perception** is defined as the ability to see, hear, or become aware of something through the senses. We take this further to say—an *increased understanding* of our experiences through that channel. In a technological world, those channels may vary and our abilities may need to be developed and honed. Our brain actually goes through different phases to help get to the "understanding" of experiences as quickly as possible. The three steps include selection, organization, and interpretation of information. (http://open.lib.umn.edu/communication/chapter/2-1-perception-process/)

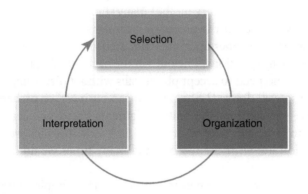

Selection is the first stage where we actually take in the information. Keep in mind we do not notice or acknowledge all of the information coming from every direction. What we actually paid attention to and absorbed is included in the selection phase. In addition, our brains determine immediate recognition of certain topics, specific people speaking, etc.; any type of trigger that could engage you to pay attention

is also included with selection. Imagine you are sitting in class, listening to your professor lecture, and taking notes over the information. Suddenly you receive an urgent text message from your boss saying you need to call him as soon as possible. More than likely, your focus shifted to the text message, wondering what your boss wants, etc. instead of paying attention to your instructor.

Now, what do you do with all of the information (because there will be a lot)? The next phase is **organization**, to arrange all of the data into different categories such as greater importance, similarity to other knowledge, our experiences, and possible issues of conflict. For example, did you ever experience a "bad feeling" after a conversation with someone? You have nothing to validate your feelings, but your gut tells you something could be trouble. Think about how you prioritize tasks to complete at work - what needs your immediate attention? what deadline is approaching quickly? You could have a "to-do" list ready to go at 9 a.m. but by 9:30 am a new task needs your focus now! Our brain goes through that same process when organizing information.

The last phase is **interpretation**, which focuses on answering the questions, "Why/How does this information matter?" Think about interpretation as the learning and storage phase of information gathering. We may try new approaches when interacting with coworkers. What types of responses did we receive—positive or negative? Did you get the feedback you expected? What would you try differently in the future? Interpreting allows us to reflect on interactions and the information processed to determine how our initial thoughts influence our own behaviors and the actions of others.

Constructs

To help us go through those phases even faster, our brain has what are called *constructs* to make those snap decisions about how we should act, how others are behaving, or to try to gain an understanding of a situation. There are four main constructs we will examine. Keep in mind each of the following constructs can be both positive and negative in nature, as we have all experienced both the pros and cons of multiple situations in communicating with others.

Prototypes

The sample, the model, or the "first" type of interaction we have. Think back to a bad class you have taken and what the instructor was like. Describe them—were they monotone? Assigned lots of "busy" work?

© sibgat/Shutterstock.com

Did not return grades in a timely manner? This would be a "**prototype**" of a bad instructor. So, when you enter a new class for the first time and you hear a monotone voice, that prototype switch flips on in your mind as a warning about your last experience. (Do not forget all the positive experiences too!)

Stereotypes

"All Texans ride horses." "Old people can't use technology." "Asians are good at math." Ever heard or made a statement similar to one of these? Unfortunately, people often use **stereotypes** to make snap judgments about others, and usually they are negative in nature. We used *preconceived notions* or information we have heard from another source, to judge a person, organization, situation, etc. Have you ever looked at teacher evaluations online to decide which teacher to take for a specific course? The deep, abstract question that derives from researching stereotypes and perception is, "Do people create stereotypes or do stereotypes create the type of people we become?"

Personal Constructions

With stereotypes, we rely on information we obtain from other sources whether it be a close friend, something we have seen portrayed in the media, etc. However, we also form assumptions based on our own experiences. This knowledge is referred to as **personal constructions**. You are the person describing your experience with that really good instructor and encouraging someone to take that class. You attended a meeting of that specific organization and are talking about what you witnessed. All the information is based on your actual involvement versus information from an outside source.

Scripts

Ever been cast in a play or performance? If so, our guess is you had a script you had to follow that included what to say, how to act, certain behaviors your character would use, etc.

© Dean Drobot/Shutterstock.com

We also have **scripts** in our everyday life that guide how we act and interact in different environments. Think about going into an interview situation; there is specific attire you wear, a pretty standard format for how an interview takes place, questions you will have to answer, and so on. There are certain behaviors we expect to occur, and when individuals act out of the ordinary (break the script), it draws our attention because it is something unexpected or out of the norm. Flash mobs are great examples of an individual or group violating the "norm" (or script) for behaviors.

Perception of Self

Understanding how the perception process works influences our ability to really understand the image we portray in our different environments such as work, home, etc. Here, we discuss the idea of the Johari Window. This theoretical construct helps people understand themselves *first* in their quest to understand others in the world around them.

Joseph Luft and Harry Ingham (Luft, 1969) as reported in Wood (2016) created the model known as "**Johari Window**" to explain how different sorts of knowledge affect self-development.

	Known to Self	Not Known to self
Known to Others	OPEN	BLIND
Not Known to Others	HIDDEN	UNKNOWN

1. The Open Area: Information known to the self and others. These are items quickly shared with others. What information are you willing to share when you first meet somebody? (Name, Major, Pets, etc.)

2. The Blind Area: Information that others know about you, but you may not know or admit to ourselves. Have you ever heard/seen a recording of yourself speaking? Maybe you did not realize you used vocal fillers (um, uh) or talk at a higher pitch on the phone, etc. That knowledge was 'blind' to you before reviewing the recording.
3. The Hidden Area: Information we know to ourselves, but keep hidden from others. Some information we may eventually share with others as we get to know and trust them; however, some facts may remain hidden permanently.
4. The Unknown Area: Possibly, the most theoretical of the four panes, this area includes things not known to others [yet] and not known to you [yet]. It may include items of potential and untapped resources.

Why it matters: In order to analyze our perceptions of others, we need to first understand how we recognize ourselves. To do this, we introduce the Johari window so students can take an introspective look at the information they believe about themselves and the things they share. Do you share too much? Do you share enough? Do your colleagues and coworkers know enough about you? What would your colleagues and coworkers say about you? You should not do this exercise to make yourself crazy, but rather to do a quick check-in to analyze the information you are sharing. Consider it a human-style "Google search" of your self-disclosure. What sort of "information" about you is "out there?" This begins a longer journey of self-awareness and emotional intelligence.

Source: Brandy Fair

It is important to understand that the Johari window panes will be different sizes for different people in your life. Look above at the figure on the left. You will see that the Unknown and Hidden panes are large compared to the other two. The first image is a good example of what the Johari window may look like when meeting someone new or your first days/weeks at a new job. You are careful with personal information, figuring out who the other people are that you are working with, learning day-to-day operations, and so on. It would be very awkward to start sharing your deep, dark secrets or telling jokes that others may find inappropriate. Now look at the figure on the right. As time passes, and you get to know and spend time with others, you begin to let down your walls and share more information about yourself and build relationships. In turn, those individuals become a great resource to provide feedback about items you did not realize about yourself (and you will know whether you can trust that person's insights too).

Many people are already quite introspective in these various areas. We introduce the Johari Window, so students of business communication can further analyze the messages they formulate and the habits they carry. For example, how do you sign your Emails? What are you wearing to work?

What would others say about what you wear to work? Have you ever considered this? Professionals' communication habits are scrutinized at every level. The various chapters of this text are designed to help students of business communication create the best and most meaningful messages in a personal and professional way.

Remember seat day? People make judgments, whether right or wrong, about others in fewer than 8 seconds—regardless of the setting. You pass people at the theme park, you notice their sports gear, and you make assumptions about what kind of fan they are. You see a woman dressed in professional business attire at the office; you make assumptions about what position she holds. If you are a fan of reality television shows, you will see many contestants withhold information or deliberately lie about their education and/or work experience to avoid other contestants judging before the competition even begins. Because assumptions are made so quickly based on perceptions, many times they are not correct. It is best to understand this, so we do not engage in the *fundamental attribution error*—where things are wrong because of other people but never ourselves. Bottom line: create the best messages, dress professional, and work to be perceived in a professional and favorable light.

Perceptions by Others

Much of the perception materials may seem similar because it operates on the same premise when compared with the communication model. What message is being sent, through which channel is it sent, and who is doing the decoding? In perceptions by others, we continue the work of self-perception by highlighting key points that may not be covered in other chapters and your other classes. We briefly discussed emails and dress, but what about timing, attitude, and behavior? What about texting, phone calls, social media? In this section of the chapter, we seek to make you aware of less common things that give off strong perception messages that run the risk of being misunderstood.

© Rido/Shutterstock.com

Berger and Calabrese (1975) as reported in Rubin and McHugh (1987) coined the **Uncertainty Reduction Theory** to illustrate how people are ". . . agents who use active, interactive, or passive strategies to reduce uncertainty. In effect, uncertainty reduction theory proposes that communication strategies are used to achieve the goal of relationship development." (p. 280). In essence, as humans we HATE the unknown. We resist change, are not really fond of surprises, and want to understand our environment as much as possible to feel comfortable and safe. This means we have to try and understand the people in our world.

Dress, Attitude, Behavior

Steve Jobs and Mark Zuckerberg are noted for their incredibly casual dress while running pinnacle American corporations. However, everyone was aware they were Chief Executive Officers long before they paid any attention to their dress. Therefore, they are not good role models of professional and practical business attire. They also come from Silicon Valley, which is highly casual and functional in its work-dress culture. It is imperative to understand the culture and dress of the world in which you are operating. This is not necessarily so that you are properly dressed and equipped to do the actual function, but more so that you will be *perceived* as capable of doing the actual function.

Some business professors require their students to attend their classes in business attire. After all, this is where you want to spend your time, and the culture of which you want to be a part. Some students push back, "It's just school," one student said. Yet, it is hard to understand why "just school" is different than, "I have to dress well for work," when in some cases you need to make favorable impressions upon your professors and colleagues at that school.

© Pixel-Shot/Shutterstock.com

The same is true for presentations. Why some students choose not to dress well for presentations boggles our minds. The whole person and the whole performance is one package. Even if you are reciting the best market plan analysis ever, you must look like you are someone who plays for the marketing team. Basketball shorts and tank tops typically do not cut it. Again, we are discussing the mitigation of misunderstandings on the part of your audience, not prejudices or thoughts that are or are not true. It is not necessarily what you say is true; rather, it is *if they believe it* to be true. You will need to make sure everything you say looks to be true to match the ethical work you did to make it as such.

Attitude and behavior fall into line with dress. While the actions you take may be true and authentic, it only matters what your receivers perceive as the truth. Take being late all the time as an example. It may be that your daycare provider is actually always the person who is late, and you tell your professor or boss, but after how many times do they think it is you and not the daycare provider? Again, it matters what others perceive. In this example, you would have to find a way to manage from the middle and create a way to be on time to convey the message you are not really a late person.

Acting professional in emails, phone calls, and text messages is also readily important. We title our text *Business Communication in a Technological World* because this is how we live. Many of the conventions of

© michaeljung/Shutterstock.com

professionalism get lost in the 144 Twitter characters, so it is important to always use greetings, closings, and the forms of good writing where necessary. These ideas are covered later in the text. Even if you are someone who never places a voice call, it is important to know what to do when someone actually answers the phone and the conventions of leaving a voicemail.

- Always greet the person and identify yourself; if leaving a voicemail, make sure to speak slowly.
- Always speak your telephone number slowly; if leaving a voicemail, make sure to repeat the number twice.
- Oftentimes a caller will leave their first name only, express it is an urgent issue, but provide no way to return their call. This often leads to a more upset individual because it now appears as if no one is returning their messages. Always remember to leave your phone number, if calling someplace that may not be a mobile phone. Some corporate phones do not have a caller ID function that matches all incoming missed calls with their numbers. Remember that the person listening to your message is writing down the information so be sure you are speaking at a pace they can follow!

Social Media

To say social media have progressed over the last several years would be an understatement. Just the way older generations approached social media then versus now is a complete change. At first, seemingly something that "kids do", social media now permeate every facet of professional life—in this technological world. Think about that. Not that long ago, you were posting weekend pictures on your MySpace where you were told by your teachers not to post anything scandalous, to today where every company, news station, and grandmother has some form of social media. Whether Etsy or Spotify, Facebook or Snapchat, TikTok or Instagram, there is a social media platform that touches your interests—what you do with it is up to you.

Why it matters? The thing to note most about social media, regardless of your intentions with their use—personal or professional, is that social media culminate in the creation of a *brand*.

How you present yourself or your business on your Instagram account is indicative of you and your brand. Are you selling the blankets you make? What do you want them to look like? Who is your target

market? In this case, your target market is your audience—your end user. The receiver. Studying who will be receiving your messages is almost, if not more important than the messages themselves.

One of the most important messages we can convey for social media is to maintain a consistent message across media and platforms so not to confuse your audience. If you use social media for professional reasons, it would be odd to then see a random political post. If you use your social media for personal reasons—friends, family, dating, it is then odd to post a group of work-related items. The most important thing above all is to evaluate what perception your audience would have if you posted this certain thing. Consider other off-putting things we see on social media: ranting, complaining, arguing, overly negative posts, too many sexually charged items, and the "isms" like racism and classism. A good rule of thumb—if you would not say it in public or at work, do not post it somewhere that is just a screen-grab away from going viral. In addition to creating your own personal brand, you also need to consider how you portray and represent your employer and the organization brand. Human Resources, your boss, etc. will probably brief you on the rules and guidelines to follow when first hired into a company. As technology continues to grow and change many companies have added verbiage or a policy about social media use. Whitfield (2013) stated, ". . . social media raises difficult questions as to whether and how rules regarding workplace loyalty, privacy, and monitoring apply to these new forums, and, if so, how these rules are balanced against freedom of expression." (p. 842). Both the organization and employer need to consider the ramifications of posting information, how the audience may interpret the message, and implementing guidelines on how/when to use social media. As an employer, Whitfield (2013) listed several steps to consider in creating a social media policy. ". . . (A) addressing social-media use in well-defined and well-communicated policies; (B) actively managing social media; (C) defining violations; and (D) updating social-media-use agreements." (p. 875). As an employee, it is your responsibility to understand if/how you may use social media, whether you may represent the organization or only yourself, and how to post without violating any company policies and face possible negative consequences.

Improving Our Perceptions

We have discussed how we make quick decisions about people, organizations, our environment, etc. We looked at how we portray ourselves and the process we go through to understand the world around us.

The only problem is we are not always correct in our initial judgments. So how can we get better at the perception process?

First and foremost, realize there is a chance you might be wrong. Do you have a person in your life who initially you did not like, but once you got to know them you became really close? Remember people do not always give off the best first impressions. What if you were having a bad day, were stressed out, feeling sick? Would that be a good first impression of who you truly are? The point is to keep in mind that your initial perception may be incorrect, so allow the person a second chance to make a good impression.

Second, be willing to do some research to learn more about a person or an organization. If one friend tells you negative things about a professor, what does the next friend say? Keep in mind one person may have had a terrible experience that is not typically the "norm" for that instructor's class. Go meet with the professor before registering for the class and gain your own perspective about them.

I can't change *yesterday*, but I can change *today*.

Finally, realize that perceptions are not concrete. Realize that people do change (depends on your perspective if it is for the good or bad). Most individuals do change with time and new experiences under their belt. If you have ever gone back to a high school reunion, you will witness the people who have moved on with their lives and now have careers, children, etc. versus those that still live the high school drama. No matter the situation, at least allow the opportunity for your perception of people to change, even if they have not.

In closing, we recognize the age-old cliché to "not worry about what people think of us," and this is good advice to help kids get through those mean years of middle school. However, in the business and technological worlds, we need not *worry* about what others think of us—but we must strive to know what it is exactly that they think. Communication professionals and professionals using communication as a tool understand the communication model. These people recognize the message they are trying to send and then speculate how it may be received.

This chapter evaluated self-perception and the perceptions others may have about us. We discussed the Johari window and the four panes of self-assessment and understanding. Moving from the self, we looked at why it is important to be aware of what messages others may be receiving about us, even if we do not intend them to be as such. While dress and behavior may be some of the most obvious nonverbal perception cues, the use of phone, email, time, and social media may be some of the lesser discussed in the perception world. To that end, make sure your personal brand is clear, consistent, and professional as you communicate across all facets of your life's channels—face-to-face and online.

REFERENCES

Rubin, R. B. & McHugh, M. P. (1987). Development of parasocial interaction relationships. *Journal of Broadcasting & Electronic Media, 31*(3), 279–292.

Whitfield, B. H. (2013). Social media @ work: #policyneeded. *Arkansas Law Review, 66*(3), 843–878.

Wood, J. (2015). *Interpersonal communication: Everyday encounters* (8th ed.). Belmont, CA: Wadsworth Publishing

© StockLite/Shutterstock.com

Most likely, you have heard a discussion somewhere that encompasses the generations all working together in an organization. Popular articles, Facebook posts, HR literature, and college campuses were all buzzing about how Millennials fit into the workplace. This topic is not new and, in many cases, no different or noteworthy than any previous generational discussions. The difference was Millennials are here *en masse* and have access to more information and media than any generation before them. Because of this, Millennials posed a daunting new cohort to the powers-that-be in the workforce: Generation X and the Baby Boomers. How does everyone work together? How do we communicate? Why are "they" (whoever they it is) so different?

Today, the conversation has evolved into a discussion of Gen Z in the workplace. This discussion, for whatever, reason, isn't as fervent as that of the Millennials that came before. This may primarily be due to the smaller number of Gen Z members, the fast their parents are younger and less worried about traditional workplace norms, or that fewer older generations are working with this cohort. Regardless the reason, Generation Z is in our colleges and work spaces, they possess their own characteristics, and will likely have jobs more affected by the Coronavirus pandemic in ways other generations may have been buffered.

What follows is a general discussion of the generational cohorts divided by age and some characteristic traits about the cohort, in general. Then, we will recognize why many of the discussions about the generations are based on stereotypes and often serve no real purpose. Finally, we will discuss business communication strategies for harmonious work between all generations.

Baby Boomers

We start our discussion here with the **Baby Boomers**, known as the cohort born between 1946 and 1964. Socially, this group saw the influx and increase of television. They experienced the Vietnam War and other military conflicts. This generation experienced the big boom of the 1980s and the older members witnessed the domestic civil rights movements of the 1960s. This generation saw a time of great American growth and change. It also saw its share of challenges: socially, politically, and financially. Baby Boomers rebelled against their Traditionalist parents when it came to sex, drugs, and rock and roll. This group has a strong work ethic, often had to fight for a place at the table with their many other brothers and sisters, and began to witness divorce and the workaholic syndrome.

© mypokcik/Shutterstock.com

Generation X

Born between 1965 and 1980, this smaller cohort became the latch-key kid generation to its Baby Boomer parents, who both were working at the office. Because of divorce, a slower economy, and other issues post–Vietnam, this generation began to trust no one and question authority. They also began to question some issues at work rooted in their own confidence and control of technology. Boomer parents had fewer children, which led to fewer **Xers**.

© Keith Bell/Shutterstock.com

Millennials

Born between 1981 and 2001, the **Millennials** are the largest American generation with roughly 84 million members. This group mostly grew up with technology and absolutely is digitally native to many platforms including video games, computers, and cell phones. Some argue that this generation was carefully wanted and curated by their parents making sure there were fewer latch-key kids and more family involvement. Thus, the generation is often regarded as having helicopter parents who have been, perhaps, too involved in their lives—often extending their adolescence. Others argue that extended Millennial adolescence is a negative stereotype and often not true, and instead the worst recession since the great depression has forced Millennials to live with their parents, taking on fewer "big" responsibilities like houses, cars, spouses, and kids—because they all cost money. This results in an appearance of desired longer term adolescence, but many scholars feel it is unfair.

© mypokcik/Shutterstock.com

At the workplace, Millennials are identified as confident, opinionated, and open-minded. They are often noted as wanting to advance without putting in the experiential work a Baby Boomer would; to which others are quick to note, they learn much more via the Internet than perhaps a Baby Boomer does using task-orientation or years on the job. Of course, when the two generations end up in the same organization, there is a potential for friction.

Generation Z

Generally considered those born in the mid-to-late nineties and not after 2010. This generation shares characteristics with the Millennials in ways it has grown up with the Internet, entertainment, and cell phones. Deloitte (2022 n.d.) offers a blog piece that suggests **Gen Z** will soon step onto the world stage and will do so seeking creative outlets and bringing with it the desire for mobile and technology use.

We argue the pandemic forced workers of all ages into understanding and in some cases, acceptance, of these characteristics. Pre-pandemic Gen Z may have interviewed for entry-level jobs via Skype or online platforms like Go-to-meeting or Zoom. Now, with the workforce a much different place and, at the time of this writing, the pandemic not completely in the past--almost all facets of life have seen technology impose a new way of doing things in order to operate during and ongoing with Covid-19.

Writing Business Communication in a Technological World underscores the notion your authors believe technology plays an integral role in communication and effective communication, regardless of its channel, is imperative to get things done. Understanding who the receivers are and who the senders are in the various communication situations will help increase the communication efficacy and effect. We hope understanding the different generations will circumvent old stereotypes and help bring fresher perspectives tho those practicing business communication.

The Stereotypes

A few years ago if you were to Google "Millennial stereotypes" or "Millennial traits" there would be lists of companies trying to understand seemingly negative characteristics of this generational cohort. When conducting a training for a large organization, the authors of your textbook asked participants to list "characteristics of their Millennial colleagues." What ensued was not limited to the list of entitled, self-centered, distracted, technology-driven, nonloyal, and on and on. In some cases, participants called out correctly the many positive characteristics of Millennial people: open-minded, progressive, desire to achieve, technology-driven. We've noticed since the research and publication of the first edition of this text, that much of the Millennial chatter has died down. This is most likely attributed to their turning 40 years old. More than half of America is a Millennial or younger. So, with this group in positions of leadership and visibility in all facets of professional life, there's less chatter about how to "deal with" or work with Millennials, and more chatter about the landscape of work in general.

Interestingly, when conducting a Google search of "Gen Z Stereotypes," many of the top line descriptions begin by describing Millennials. Conversely, when we performed this search for Millennials 10 years ago, the discussion didn't start by mentioning Gen X. A further inspection does less to warrant negative stereoptypes of Gen Z and more to compare and contrast them to Millennials. Additionally, almost all characteristics of Gen Z mention their interpersonal use of technology. This is something to consider when working with clients and colleagues across all generations. Notice we mention technology-driven again. It is for this reason, we author the following section "History is Written by the Victors."

History Is Written by the Victors

As events go, it is commonly noted that whomever "wins" the war "writes" the history book of that event—the players, who was right and wrong, and why. Think about American history books. Ever wonder how the story of the American Revolution is told in Great Britain? We argue the same can be said for the narrative that is shaped around Millennials and Generzation Z in the workplace. As that cohorts began going to work in the middle to late 2000s, there were more Boomers and Xers in charge at those organizations. Encountering Millennial workers—fewer in number and who had different styles of working and learning—led to a larger stereotype: entitled, lazy, etc. What if it was a case of history being written by the victors—and in this case, at that time, the "victors" were the generations with more workers and larger stages from which to make stories, and less about what was really happening with the shifting work culture.

Stereotypes of the Shifting Work Culture

Much of the Millennial discussion was not new in form. When Boomer women arrived in the workplace, there was pushback. When Xer "slackers" and questioners of authority arrived in the workplace, they too were called lazy at first. The situation with the Millennials was no different. The major difference is there are more of them. Millennials, large in number, were quick to enter the workplace and caused the generational cohort discussion to occur quickly. So quickly, in fact, that many employers began studying the Millennial population. These employers asked questions like: How can we recruit Millennials? What are their working preferences? Do we have an environment that fosters a solid work–life balance? There seems to be less of a push with Generation Z in regards to studying and/or recruiting them to work for organizations. What may alter this understanding is the pandemic. Ripples from Covid have affected and will continue to affect facets of personal and professional lives.

Employers asked these questions because they were finding that Millennials were "job hopping"—that is, changing jobs when they were dissatisfied with a working situation. Some of the larger corporations would onboard Millennial employees spending time and resources to train them, only to have them leave when the practices of the organization left the Millennials feeling that the picture painted during the hiring process was not the true picture of what really happened at the company. For this example, we must consider work–life balance. Coming from the workaholic culture of the 80s and 90s, it was expected that employees would work 50–60 hours a week for a company. The Millennials have slowly put an end to this. Something that the Xers began with maternity leave policies and telecommuting. However, now, when Millennials are told one thing in the hiring process (You will work 40 hours a week) and then something else happens (You need to stay this weekend and work)—the Millennials have found it easier simply to leave a company rather than argue with authority. Additionally, some articles comment on how "younger" workers from Gen Z will "ghost" a company. That is, not show up for interviews or work; or take a job only to stop coming. Often these articles have an "offended tone," where the writer feels the ghosting is inappropriate or disrespectful. And, in some cases, it may be. However, it might be time for older generations to realize a young person does not want to be paid minimum wage to sit someplace when they can make and sell their own products online. It doesn't seem fair anymore to ask younger workers to dress up nicely only to pay them a wage that would take them three weeks to earn the cost of a shirt from the mall. It's not our goal to get into social commentary about wage gaps and experience in America. However, the pandemic taught us quite quickly that technology and telecommunication could actually happen when for so long the older generations were reluctant. Who's to say the same isn't true now with ghosting, poor pay, and the changing landscape of work.

© mypokcik/Shutterstock.com

Therefore, we encourage our business communication students to be careful of stereotypes as they pertain to all people. It is nothing new that changing demographics create growing pains when new generations join a workplace. It *is* new that with the rise of social media and size of the current generation, more people are talking about the clash of generations at the workplace. We cannot stress enough this was happening before; now, it is getting "more media." We also encourage employees of all generations to have an open mind when working with others. It is possible that a bad worker is simply a bad worker, not because of their age—but simply because they are not a good worker. Continuously defining work ethic by age encourages rote division based on demographics and not character.

Business Communication Strategies

Understanding Your Audience

It is pretty likely you are reading this book as part of a speech class or a communication course that has speeches and presentations. To that end, one of the most important things a speaker learns is the necessity to curtail one's message to his or her audience. With whatever resources are available, it is absolutely necessary to try as much as possible to curate a message for the intended receivership, so that it is best understood. Talking in jargon, colloquialisms, or language unknown to a general audience will quickly lose their attention and ultimately the action you wish them to make. This same principle should be applied to interorganizational and cross-organizational communication. We will explain here.

The Stuff "Old People" Do

Remember the fax machine? Yeah, neither do we! Well, that is not entirely true because occasionally we are forced to use it for professional or personal reasons. In one case, while teaching at our current universities, we were each required to request transcripts from our previous colleges using a fax machine. In another instance, we were required to fax those transcripts to someone else because an email was deemed "unsafe." Or, how about how we just spelled email? Countless colleagues older than your author team still insist there needs to be a hyphen in the word email. We argue why? Everyone knows what we're talking about, so why add the extra character of the hyphen, especially when in Twitter and other platforms characters are limited?

The truth of the matter is if we wanted those transcripts we needed to figure out a fax machine—as that was what our audience requested. Moreover, if the editor of our journal articles wanted a hyphen—we gave her a hyphen. The point here is to do what is necessary to get the message across and ultimately what you are seeking. Sure, we can dig our heels in and complain about "old people," but if it is not too hard to play by the set rules, why not? (Within reason. The whole lack of male paternity leave or firing someone because of race and gender stuff had to stop).

The Basics

Throughout this book, different sections highlight various communication tools and channels for operation in a business and technological world. Usually, this includes learning many of the basics of business communication and technical writing. For example, it is good to learn the traditional way to formulate a resume. Sure, technological advances have the possibility of making resumes flashy and pretty, but remember your audience. Understand a few things: Are you applying to a traditionally conservative field e.g., banking, accounting, finance, economics? Are you applying to a large multinational corporation that needs a simple Word or PDF file that can be easily translated to HTML language for an inner-office hiring system? Is it possible your bosses may be of a different, and possibly more traditional, generation or country than you?

Another example is cover letters and business letters. Regardless of the channel: email, paper mail, printed documents, it is important to know the conventions of beautiful and professional business letter writing. There is no denying that letters of years prior, before the digital age, were much longer in nature because it took more time and more effort to exchange information. Think snail mail and typewritten letters. Now, even though emails can be exchanged as fast as text messages via a phone, it is still important to seek to understand your target audience. If your audience is of a generation that uses business letters, business letterhead, and standard English conventions, it is probably good to write to their style and taste—especially, if they are your client.

A good place to practice style and taste is at the college level. Often, professors require things students deem outdated: typed papers, formal phone calls, proper emails. While these things may not be commonplace in the artistic, creative, and Millennial or Gen Z worlds for all, it is necessary to understand the audience, know what you are seeking (advice, guidance, an A), and continue accordingly. This practice is good for the move from college to industry.

© Pera Nikolic/Shutterstock.com

Beyond Basics

As communication specialists, we strive to mention many aspects of the business communication experience in order to help our students achieve maximum understanding and success in their endeavors. We title this section ***Beyond Basics*** because of the nuances surrounding the modes of communication listed below. To many, the telephone (actually talking on it and leaving voice mail) are basic communication traits. Yet, we hear from faculty and business people across the United States that younger people are not using the phone and voice mail as much as in prior years. We use Beyond Basics because for some, the paradigm of what was once basic is now the norm—or the new basic. For your authors, we prefer a quick text message than a lengthy voice mail. Yet, more traditional people consider this too casual. Furthermore, some consider texting for personal reasons and voice mail for professional. We offer some insight here.

First, you guessed it—consider your audience! Who are you trying to reach? What are you trying to do? Is the phone number you have a business line? Perhaps match a voice mail with an email to ensure a unified delivery and for follow-up. In emails, letters, and websites, seek to understand how the person would like to be contacted.

Second, what is the purpose of your communication? Are you trying to work on something with someone whom you have already established a relationship? If so, you should probably consider a phone call. Many times, a 5-minute phone call can handle something far easier than dozens of emails exchanged over hours or days. We see this when working with students. After the third email about a project or presentation, it is far easier to meet with a student; or *call* them to chat, rather than explain things in an email.

Familiarize yourself with conventions of phone calls. We know, we know—this seems elementary. Is it? Have you role-played calling a business with your parents or friends? In the 2020s, it is more likely than ever before that students have not rehearsed business calls with anyone. Why would they when many things are handled on the Internet, and companies like Bank of America and United Airlines make it nearly impossible to find their phone numbers when you as a customer want to reach them. Major corporations push so many formerly phone-called conversations to the Web that it is no wonder that many people do not use the phone.

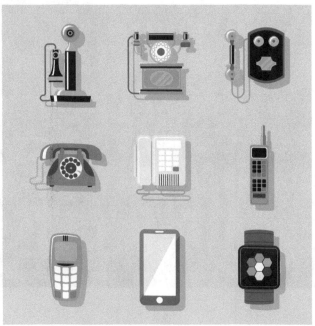

© MSSA/Shutterstock.com

We mention this not in a patronizing way, but in a way that allows all readers here to understand the shift in basics to beyond basics. Therefore, if you do call someone and they do happen to answer, make sure you are ready to say, "Hello there. I'm trying to reach so-and-so." Or, "Hi my name is Chris and I'm calling for Sarah Jones." We also caution you to be aware of the title and role of the people you are calling. Professors, doctors, and people in the C-suite of a company should be addressed in the most formalized way possible with their degreed titles. People you are calling for sales, cold calls, and clients should be referred to in the cultural formalities, if their ages and titles are unknown: Mr. and Ms. Lateral calls and when addressing people of your same experience, education, and rank, it is typically appropriate and expected to use their first name or first and last name. We note it is a bit odd for a mid-level employee at one bank calling another bank to work on a project and using the title of Ms. Jones. It sounds more authoritative and professional to say, "Hi this is Steve Smith and I'm calling for Sarah Jones." Again, always refer back to the scope of your audience.

© MichaelJayBerlin/Shutterstock.com

When Generations Clash

We note as Generation Xers, there may be times when someone from another generational cohort makes comments, inferences, or assumptions about work ethic that is inaccurate. Being professors in the 2000s, it was not uncommon for our more senior colleagues to say we looked like kids, or to do things that seemed inefficient to us—like—not using course management systems, etc. We saw technological conflict at our institutions when online courses and other online platforms were introduced and the different generations were not all in agreement on their uses. So, we get it. We offer a few suggestions to defeat and deflect workplace stereotypes from all angles . . . Boomer on down and Gen Z on up.

1. Let your work do the talking. Sometimes, there are assumptions made about how hard we work. Turn assumptions into realities with documented proof, attained deadlines, and beautiful outcomes.
2. Talk to people. If your ideas are overlooked or not heard, set meetings and follow-up with people, so they know that you too have ideas.
3. Use the most direct means of communication to have the most direct conversations. If someone slights you in a meeting, or if you want to congratulate someone—discuss both situations with

© Ditty_about_summer/Shutterstock.com

someone on the phone. Or, if you would like a paper trail, consider formalized, well-written email correspondence. Be careful with the emails and make sure you realize that *everything is public* regardless of how many times and places you write "confidential."

4. Always be professional, not necessarily cold, but never casual. Make sure you create credibility so people take you seriously. This can include dress, the way you address someone, and your writing. Many are considered casual dressers in the workplace, but we feel this affects all generations. There are some pretty outdated, ill-fitting outfits adorning some Boomers out there.

5. Seek mentorship and guidance. If you run into communication problems with someone from another generation or work ethic, seek advice from someone else in that cohort or situation. This may provide perspective on how to work with that person.

We have discussed the generational cohorts, the stereotypes that surround them, and some techniques to move beyond those stereotypes. It cannot be stressed enough to understand your audience when dealing with intergenerational colleagues and coworkers. There are many books, articles, and blogs written about the generations in the workplace. This chapter spent some time discussing the narrative around Millennials and Generation Z because many college students fall into this cohort and many nontraditional-aged students manage and employ this cohort. We seek to bring enlightenment and perspective to everyone in an organization, so work can be effective and enjoyable and filled with purpose, and not conflict, over communication styles.

General cohort information from *Sticking Points* by Haydn Shaw, 2013; Generation Z years from Google indexing.

REFERENCE

Shaw, H. (2013). *Sticking points: how to get 4 generations working together in the 12 places they come apart.* Carol Stream, IL: Tyndale House Publishers.

5 Verbal Communication

Chapter Overview
Verbal Communication Defined

When creating a message, it is important to consider what you are saying and also *how* you say it. Effective verbal communication is clear and delivered in a way that aligns with the receiver's expectation. In the workplace, verbal communication should follow the basic principles of etiquette. How you speak influences someone's impression of you; thus, it's important to always be professional and polite. The Willingness to Communicate Scale (WTC; McCroskey, 1992; McCroskey & Richmond 1987) measures an individual's enthusiasm to communicate in public, meetings, and in group settings with strangers, acquaintances, and friends. To better understand how often you choose to communicate in these settings take the quiz.

Willingness to Communicate (WTC)

Willingness to communicate is the most basic orientation toward communication. Almost anyone is likely to respond to a direct question, but many will not continue or initiate interaction. This instrument measures a person's willingness to *initiate* communication. The face validity of the instrument is strong, and results of extensive research indicate the predictive validity of the instrument. Alpha reliability estimates for this instrument have ranged from 0.85 to well above 0.90. Of the 20 items on the instrument, eight are used to distract attention from the scored items. The twelve remain items generate a total score, four context-type scores, and three receiver-type scores. The sub-scores generate lower reliability estimates, but generally high enough to be used in research studies.

   Directions: Below are 20 situations in which a person might choose to communicate or not to communicate. Presume you have completely free choice. Indicate the percentage of times you would choose to communicate in each type of situation. Indicate in the space at the left of the item what percent of the time you would choose to communicate. (0 = Never to 100 = Always)

_____1. Talk with a service station attendant.

_____2. Talk with a physician.

_____3. Present a talk to a group of strangers.

_____4. Talk with an acquaintance while standing in line.

_____5. Talk with a salesperson in a store.

_____6. Talk in a large meeting of friends.

_____7. Talk with a police officer.

_____8. Talk in a small group of strangers.

_____9. Talk with a friend while standing in line.

_____10. Talk with a waiter/waitress in a restaurant.

_____11. Talk in a large meeting of acquaintances.

_____12. Talk with a stranger while standing in line.

_____13. Talk with a secretary.

_____14. Present a talk to a group of friends.

_____15. Talk in a small group of acquaintances.

_____16. Talk with a garbage collector.

_____17. Talk in a large meeting of strangers.

_____18. Talk with a spouse (or girl/boyfriend).

_____19. Talk in a small group of friends.

_____20. Present a talk to a group of acquaintances.

Scoring:
Context-type sub-scores–
Group Discussion: Add scores for items 8, 15, and 19; then divide by 3.
Meetings: Add scores for items 6, 11, 17; then divide by 3.
Interpersonal: Add scores for items 4, 9, 12; then divide by 3.
Public Speaking: Add scores for items 3, 14, 20; then divide by 3.

Receiver-type sub-scores–
Stranger: Add scores for items 3, 8, 12, 17; then divide by 4.
Acquaintance: Add scores for items 4, 11, 15, 20; then divide by 4.
Friend: Add scores for items 6, 9, 14, 19; then divide by 4.
To compute the total WTC score, add the sub scores for stranger, acquaintance, and friend. Then divide by 3.

All scores, total and sub-scores, will fall in the range of 0 to 100
Norms for WTC Scores:
Group discussion >89 High WTC, <57 Low WTC
Meetings >80 High WTC, <39 Low WTC
Interpersonal conversations >94 High WTC, <64 Low WTC
Public Speaking >78 High WTC, <33 Low WTC
Stranger >63 High WTC, <18 Low WTC
Acquaintance >92 High WTC, <57 Low WTC
Friend >99 High WTC, <71 Low WTC
Total WTC >82 High Overall WTC, <52 Low Overall WTC

As you analyze your answers consider how region impacts your comfort level when talking to a station attendant. There are only a few places in the United States where you are legally not allowed to pump your own gas. If you are from one of those locations, you might feel more comfortable chatting with a service station attendant than someone who has not encountered that situation. Similarly, Annetee Lareau (2000) studied the behavior of children to compare how economic status influences a child's ability to communicate. By shadowing families, she found that children from wealthier families felt more confident and comfortable communicating with physicians. Specially, Lareau's research noted that wealthy parents encouraged their children to prepare questions to ask their doctors and discouraged shyness. In what ways did your upbringing impact your current comfort level when communicating with physicians? Do you feel confident to ask questions? Or do you find going to the doctor's to be overwhelming? Furthermore, how does your response differ depending on the doctor? Is it easier to communicate with your dentist than your eye doctor? As you go through each scenario in the WTC quiz consider the origin of your confidence or apprehension.

As noted in the WTC quiz, context can influenceyour ability to communicate with confidence. You might have also noticed this in your classes. Each of your professors communicates differently and that influences how students participate in class. Your math class is most likely different than your communication class. The same difference applies to the workplace, as the culture of the environment is influenced by the behavior and expectations of managers and bosses. Much of this was discussed in the chapter on work culture. Thus, while you practice professional verbal communication it is important to observe and consider your environment to determine what is appropriate. The following sections explain how language is symbolic, cultural, and can evolve. As a refresher: **verbal communication** includes written and spoken language. **Nonverbal communication** includes the alternative ways messages are conveyed—through gestures, dress, etc.

Language is Symbolic

Language is symbolic because it provides a framework for groups of people to communicate their culture, and idea or concept. Symbols can be as basic as a cross representing your belief in Christianity, a Greek symbol that identifies what sorority or fraternity you're in, or even a brand's logo. However, depending on the context the symbol is used there might be different meanings. For example, the swastika has been a symbol used by various cultures for centuries in India, China, Africa, and native America before it was used to represent Nazi extremism. Despite its history, if you were to see a swastika today you would connect the symbol to White Supremacy and fascism. Similarly, the cartoon figure of Pepe the Frog from the comic "Boy's Life" is now considered a hate symbol by The Southern Poverty Law Center since the racist anti-Semitic alt-right movement converted the image into a meme on platforms such as 4chan, 8chan, and Reddit. However, symbols are contextual. In the United States Pepe is shown wearing a Hitler-like moustache but in Hong Kong Pepe is a symbol of rebellion against the Chinese government. Thus, language and symbols are culturally contextual.

In the workplace symbols matter because they are socially shared images. For example, a logo influences how the organization is branded to the public. Consider your favorite products, in what ways does just the symbol of their logo create an emotional appeal for you? What does the logo communicate? Certain words are also socially shared and can also provide the same emotional response. For example, if you use or do not use your co-worker preferred pronouns you are communicating a message beyond, she, he, or they. A single word can shift the way the receiver understands your message. Furthermore, there are certain words that are considered inappropriate regardless of the context simply because the word itself symbolizes something. Consider the language you use at work, in class, or among different groups of friends. What words would make symbolic sense in one setting but be confusing in another?

© 5DN1L/Shutterstock.com

Language is Cultural

Since language is symbolic, words and behavior are not universally understood. If a student who grew up in the UK and studies abroad in the United States askes her classmate for a "rubber" it would not be universally understood that she is referring to an eraser. Not only might the student receive an object she did not request but the context of the conversation has shifted. Language is not only influenced by geographical differences but also gender, religion, and age.

The way we speak is influenced by cultural characteristics, patterns, and customs.

Language Evolves

Language in our lives
Personal Lives
Professional Lives

Organizations need to consider how language influences the interpersonal relationships between the organization and employees, how language impacts the relationships employees have with customers, and lastly, how language influences the perception of the organization to external audiences. First, employers might use what is known as *personal* language, or "we" language, to establish a close-knit workplace culture. For example, "At Wilford Industries, we appreciate all our ticketed passengers." Whereas "Wilford Industries appreciates it's ticketed passengers" disconnects the organization from the passengers. Another example of *impersonal* language is "employees" or "members" instead of "we" or "us." Using personal language is mostly seen in organizations the frame themselves as "one big family." The goal of this type of language is to invite employees to have an emotional investment in the organization's success.

In large organizations language and context can also influence an employee's perception. For example, the term "customer" might refer to potential customers in the sales department but in the finance department "customer" is the person who receives an invoice. Thus, the relationship between the department and the customer is different for sales and finance. The term "the customer is always right" would not be an appropriate moto in in the finance department. Lastly, how an organization frames the customer in their mission statement also matters. For example, non-profit organizations are shifting away from the word "charity" as it can be interpreted two different ways. Using the term charity to frame an organizational image or in mission statement can be viewed as helping others or engaging in a philanthropic cause. However, charity can also belittle the community the organization is attempting to help. Consider how the term "charity case" frames the person receiving aid as helpless. Instead, incorporating language from the for-profit sector, such as the word "client" or "customer" would be the more appropriate word choice and create a more balanced relationship between an organization's department the person they are assisting. Imagine a customer service department calling customers "charity cases" simply because they need assistance. Overall, language influences workplace culture and relationships.

Verbal language is important because in many written forms you have the potential to intrigue, include, intervene, invoke—and several other "i words." What's important to remember is language and verbal communication is highly grounded in context. When communication for business and the professions is at hand, or writing in a technological format, it's always important to consider (1) Who is my receiver? (2) What do I want to convey? (3) What is the format for displaying this (public, private, Email, social media, etc.), (4) Does it look professional? and (5) Can it be forwarded? Answering just a few of these questions can work toward McCroskey's Willingness to Communicate. When in doubt ask someone to pre-read verbal communication if the possibility arises. Good luck!

REFERENCES

Lareau, A. (2000). Social class and the daily lives of children: A study from the United States. *Childhood*, 7(2), 155–171.

McCroskey, J. C. (1992). Reliability and validity of the willingness to communicate scale. *Communication Quarterly, 40*, 16–25.

McCroskey, J. C., & Richmond, V. P. (1987). Willingness to communicate. In J. C. McCroskey & J. A. Daly (Eds.), *Personality and interpersonal communication* (pp. 119–131). Sage.

Chapter
6 Nonverbal Communication

It is the first day of summer school bright and early on a Monday morning in June. All of the students, minus one, are all in their seats ready to begin class so they can get out and enjoy the summer sun. The professor starts the lesson and twenty minutes into it the missing student, Katie, appears. She stumbles into her seat and stares down at the desk with her arms crossed. A frown is on her face, and her hair is disheveled. The professor takes all of this in and likely assumes the student is going to be a poor student since she did not care enough about the class to be on time. Her classmates may perceive her to be a slacker based on her sloppy appearance and won't want to work with her on group projects in the future.

We probably have all misinterpreted a situation by misreading someone's body language. This is more common than you realize. Most of how we communicate is, in fact, nonverbal. It is a common assumption among new communication scholars that communication refers to spoken words only. However, by this point in your journey through this textbook, you have likely realized there is a lot more that goes into how we transmit messages to others. The process of communication involves much more than just our words. In fact, most of what we communicate is not transmitted by our words at all. One's facial expressions or even eye contact can tell us a lot of information. Due to the considerable amount on nonverbal communication that we all use, this chapter will explore the characteristics of nonverbal communication, the types, and provide you some tips to consider that may help you enhance your own nonverbal communication.

Characteristics
Nonverbal Communication is Ambiguous

Student Katie works two jobs to pay for school. She was late to class because she worked the late shift the night before. As a result, she missed her alarm and woke up late on the first day of the summer class. She rode her bike while riding to class which messed up her hair. She also didn't have time to eat breakfast so she is frowning as her stomach is growling. Katie is also a very dedicated student, and she is avoiding looking at anyone because she is embarrassed to be late on the first day of class.

Katie's story is quite familiar to teachers everywhere. When students come to class late, there could be a variety of reasons. Some teachers assume the student does not care about the class, and by showing up late the student is demonstrating a lack of respect. However, perhaps the student had car problems or a last minute emergency that delayed them. A student looking down or not looking at the instructor may indicate either a lack of attention toward the subject or as the story above indicates, embarrassment. Even someone disheveled hair could be a result of either laziness or a sudden breeze that blew at the student as they were walking into the building. This is why nonverbal communication can be tricky to navigate, because it may be interpreted differently by different people. Katie's bad morning and resulting appearance, timing, facial expressions, and lack of eye contact all influence her professor's and classmates' perception of her.

Nonverbal communication may have **more than one meaning** depending on who is receiving it. Another classic example is a boyfriend and girlfriend having a fight. The girlfriend may cross her arms and say, "I'm fine." Her verbal communication is positive, but her nonverbal does not quite match. Some observers would argue that she is not in fact "fine." Pay special attention when someone's verbal messages do not match their nonverbal signals.

As such, as a sender of nonverbal messages you should be careful not to send confusing signals. For example, during a presentation if you tightly grip your notes, your audience may view this as you being nervous. Monitor your forms of nonverbal communication, particularly in presentations, by being aware of the many different forms of nonverbal communication. As a receiver of messages, you should think about the many different meanings that nonverbal communication could mean before you jump to any assumptions.

Connected to Our Culture

Kendra is on a business trip to Japan. She works at an electronics distributor in the United States and is in Tokyo to meet the product manufacturer to learn about some new designs. She has never traveled to Japan before and she is very excited. In her haste to leave on her trip, she does not research Japanese business customs. She arrives at her first meeting and extends her hand to her Japanese counterpart, Aiko. Aiko bows instead. Embarrassed, Kendra tries to bow, but instead knocks heads with Aiko.

Nonverbal communication is tied to our culture just as much as our spoken language. Some cultures rely heavily on nonverbal communication and subtle cues to transmit messages. Others, like the United States are more direct and use verbal language to communicate. Think about movies or television shows based in foreign countries. How do others say, "Hello" or greet each other? In countries like France, people

© Asier Romero/Shutterstock.com

use kisses on the cheek to greet each other whereas in the United States, most individuals verbally greet each other or shake hands. Kendra's mistake above was not in researching nonverbal communication or customs before travelling overseas. Even something like the amount of eye contact used with others varies depending on the culture you are in.

Another example of how nonverbal communication is tied to one's culture can be seen with gestures. Take for example, the peace symbol. In the United States two fingers in the air represent peace, but if you are in the United Kingdom and flip your fingers around, you are actually flipping someone "off." Something as small as the positioning of two fingers can mean "peace" or "F you" depending on one's culture.

Nonverbal Communication can be Intentional or Unintentional

In some of the examples noted above, the nonverbal messages were unintentional. For example, Katie's disheveled appearance certainly was not her intention. Rather it was a result of her riding her bike to school. No doubt she was not even aware that her hair was messed up. No one wants to look bad on the first day of school! Her frown was not signaling unhappiness with the professor but was a mere reflection of her own hunger and dissatisfaction with her morning.

A lot of speakers let their public speaking anxiety or nerves take over during their presentations. It can be difficult to monitor your nonverbal messages when you are nervous or trying to recall complicated content in your presentation. Oftentimes, we send involuntary messages to our audience that may be misinterpreted. For example, nerves may manifest in a speaker by the speaking swaying or shifting their weight. The audience may perceive this as being unprepared for the presentation, but really the speaker did not intend to send that message whatsoever. The first step in improving our nonverbal messages in presentations is to learn what nonverbal communication is and then being more mindful of it—even when standing nervously presenting in front of an audience

Other examples above may have been more intentional in nature. For example, Kendra extending her hand as a greeting was a purposeful action that unfortunately had adverse consequences. You can use nonverbal signals strategically while at the same time avoiding mistakes like Kendra made. A well placed gesture during a presentation can add emphasis or importance to your verbal statements. In the United States making eye contact with your audience signals to them that you are prepared for the presentation and are confident in public speaking.

© Fractal Pictures/Shutterstock.com

When preparing your professional presentations, consider all of the various forms of nonverbal communication outlined below. Small strategic adjustments can send positive messages to your audience. Use your knowledge of nonverbal communication to enhance your presentation and not detract from it. Plan out some movement, dress professionally, and be mindful of your nervous behaviors.

Nonverbal Communication Fills in the Blanks

Meredith is having coffee with her new colleague Patrick. Patrick asks about the work culture and Meredith gives him an extended pause and a look. From this, Patrick perceives there may be some drama going on at the office.

If something is not said using verbal communication or words, often a communication receiver can rely on nonverbal to fill in the blanks. Some things are better expressed through a facial expression or gesture than by using actual words. Maybe Patrick asks her how the parking is at the office since they share a parking lot with another business. Meredith simply shrugs her shoulders. From this, Patrick can ascertain there are some parking struggles.

Also, nonverbal signals can reinforce messages that are transmitted. If Meredith says, "I don't know about the parking" while shrugging her shoulders, the gesture reinforces her verbal message. Adding nonverbal messages to a verbal message can help repeat the central idea.

Nonverbal Communication is Powerful

Kory is at his very first auction while attending a non-profit fundraising event. He is given a paddle with the number 25 on it. He sits down and watches as the auction host brings out various expensive items. Bidding begins. Suddenly, Kory sees his best friend Glen and excitedly waives at him. The auctioneer sees Kory's paddle and says, "Sold to number 25! A beautiful set of crystal ducks for $1,000!" Shocked, Kory lowers his paddle and starts thinking how he is going to explain this to his wife.

Based on everything mentioned above, it is evident that nonverbal communication is powerful. Let's be honest, all communication is powerful. But, what makes nonverbal special is how meaningful messages can be! A single gesture can cost someone a thousand bucks (or get him some ducks!) (see Kory above). Another gesture can royally offend someone. Not giving attention to nonverbal messages, let's say at the start of a meeting, could derail negotiations if you are not careful. Sending the wrong nonverbal messages while in a foreign country could also land you in trouble.

Think about a time in your life when you were in an argument with someone. What was their nonverbal communication? Standing with your arms crossed, raising your voice, or scrunching your face all are pretty strong indicators of displeasure. Again, all communication is powerful, but there is something uniquely potent about nonverbal communication. So let's shift gears and learn about the different types of nonverbal in hopes of making you more aware of your own communication practices.

Types of Nonverbal Communication

Prepare to have your mind blown! You may be thinking the nonverbal communication is simply your body language or things that you do with your face. In fact, there are many types of nonverbal communication you may not have considered before. The types below first reflect the types of nonverbal communication that we generally think of relating to our own body or persons. However, as you are about to find out, there are other categories of nonverbal communication that includes your environment or even inanimate objects!

© Mary Swift/Shutterstock.com

Oculesics

Oculesics is the term used to refer to eye contact or how our eyes communicate. Direct or indirect eye contact can transmit messages. When asked by his mother whether or not he ate all of the cookies, 6-year-old Henry looked down at the floor and said nothing. The avoidance of making eye contact clearly reflects his guilt and that he was the original cookie monster.

In addition to reflecting guilt, eye contact can also transmit a very direct and clear message. For example, Brandie is at a fancy work party, but after a long day at the office she is ready to leave the party and head home. She looks at her boyfriend James and makes eye contact. A quick sideways glance at the door and instantly James knows she is ready to leave.

Some cultures use eye contact in different ways. Eye contact may indicate a sign or respect and in some cultures, are required to have a meaningful conversation. Alternatively, in some countries perhaps it is impolite to make direct eye contact with your superior at work. This is where careful research and planning before travel can come in handy so that you are not offended if someone is speaking to you, but not making direct eye contact with you.

What is Callie the dog's eye contact saying? Does she want to eat or does she see a squirrel?

Vocal Qualities

There is a difference between your words and how you say them or your voice. Your words are forms of verbal communication. Recall from previous chapters that verbal communication and language are just symbols used to express ideas. However, these are different than *how you say them*. This includes things such as volume, pace, tone, pronunciation, and even the use of vocal fillers such as "uh" or "um." It is fair to say that when a speaker pauses and uses an "uh" that they are not in fact trying to intentionally communicate.

Imagine one day your professor comes to class and is speaking in a slow manner that is unusual for them. This nonverbal signal may reflect that they are tired or are having a bad day. Alternatively, imagine your professor walks into class speaking extra loudly that day. Did they drink too much coffee? Are they mad at the class? This highlights not only the power of nonverbal communication like your voice, but also the ambiguous nature of it.

Facial Expression

Notice that eye contact is in a separate category than facial expressions. This is because a person can be smiling at you, but also avoiding making eye contact at the same time. Our faces show a lot! Emotion is one thing that is frequently transmitted through our facial expressions. For example, Stephen is out to a fancy dinner with his friend Lacey and he orders escargot. He doesn't realize that escargot is actually a French dish consisting of snails. He takes a large bite and realizes instantly that this dish is not the one for him. How would he communicate that to his friend Lacey without words (since his mouth is full of snail)? You guessed it, through his facial expressions. Our faces show disgust, joy, sadness, anger, contempt, or even pleasure. As referenced above, sometimes this is intentional and other times our faces may communicate something unintentional. Even something as simple as a smile can make a presenter feel more welcoming and inviting.

© lassedesignen/Shutterstock.com

Kinesics or Body Language

Let's go back to that fancy work party where Brandie and James are. Although it is in the ballroom of a nice hotel (with a build your own ice cream sundae bar), do you think you could identify who is enjoying the party and who is not based solely on their body language? Co-worker Matt is nervously shifting his weight from foot to foot and keeps looking at his watch. Senior manager Mark is standing with his arms crossed, with the exception of the occasional yawn. Are they enjoying themselves or have they had enough of the desserts and are ready to head home? Our body language says a lot about what we are thinking and how we are feeling about something.

Gestures

Gestures are referenced above, but this is one of those areas of nonverbal communication to mindful of when traveling overseas. You do not want to accidentally offend someone by giving the wrong gesture. Carefully research gestures and their meanings when travelling.

In the realm of public speaking, gestures are great! A well placed gesture can keep your audience engaged and interested in your subject. Something as simple as counting on your fingers will help your audience follow along with your main points. Gestures can also **add emphasis** to what you are speaking about. Imagine you are at an event on campus with a local politician giving a passionate speech full of emotion about the pollution in your area. Now imagine the speaker is standing there with her hands down at her sides the entire presentation. Does the picture of her standing there motionless match the passion in her voice? She should use gestures to highlight how bad the pollution situation is and to encourage change.

Be mindful of what you are using because there is gesture overload. Too many wild gestures will make you look extremely nervous or even like the wacky waving inflatable arm guy. A prepared speaker will rehearse their presentation with gestures to see what the best signals for the message being delivered are.

Many common gestures in business and interpersonal relationships were altered during the Covid pandemic. At first people didn't know if they should shake hands. Then there was the fist-bump which people deemed "safer" for some reason. Lest we not forget the touching of elbows among friends, and there was often a wave hello from a car. Think about these "alternative" greetings to the traditional handshake. Much like we discuss in other chapters, the message is intentionally the same, but the channel and/or the encoding of the message was altered.

© Keegan Divant/Shutterstock.com

Posture

Posture is one of those important nonverbal signals we rarely think about when giving a professional presentation or communicating in general. For those of us who are natural slouchers, this is bad news. Unfortunately, people with bad posture may be associated with being lazy or not caring. Now, we are not suggesting you take an etiquette class where you have to walk laps while balancing a book on your head. But, be aware that a hunched over posture during a presentation may signal that you are uncomfortable or unprepared for the presentation even if the opposite is true.

Ambiguous signals from posture does not just impact presentations, but may impact your communication in other situations. Imagine you are a hiring partner at an accounting firm. Do you want to hire a recent college graduate who is sitting hunched over or one that is sitting straight up and great eye contact? Or you are going on your first Tinder date and you walk into the restaurant only to find someone sitting there looking down with their shoulders curled forward. You may start to think he or she is not even interested in getting to know you. Having a confident and open posture sends welcoming signals to others. It also makes an audience view you as a confident expert in the subject you are presenting on.

Touch

Touch is a very important sense to humans and through touch we signal not just our feelings, but also the closeness of the relationship. Think for a moment about how you greet people that you meet in business. You likely shake hands and keep touch to a minimum. But, say you are greeting a family member or a close friend that you have not seen in a long time, you may opt for a hug with a squeeze. We tend to touch those that we have closer or intimate relationships with.

Touch also can transmit emotions or feelings. Take Sean, a professional gamer. When Sean loses at a professional gaming tournament, his friend Chris goes up and gives him a pat on the back. That pat signals Chris understands and feels sympathy for Sean's loss. Or let's say Sean wins! Maybe he gets a high five! This gesture combined with touch signals celebration and a congratulations on the win. Take mental notes for the next two days and see who you make physical contact with in your life. It will likely be your close friends or romantic partner, not necessarily a random classmate that you have never spoken to.

© Rido/Shutterstock.com

Environmental

It is your first day working at a telecommunications company. Before you are even introduced to your boss or anyone else at the company, from looking around you will be able to learn a lot about the individuals working there. For example, the employees who have their own individual private offices likely are higher up than those in the middle of the floor in cubicles. Additionally, who generally occupies the corner office? That's right, the big dog.

You may even walk down the hall where a bunch of professors' offices are located. One professor's office is full of books and is messy, another's is very tidy with few personal objects, and the third has magazines and a coffee machine available for students. The way we place objects or display them in spaces can

© thodonal88/Shutterstock.com

---

10 Tips for Strong Nonverbal Signals while Presenting

Tip 1: Maintain eye contact with your audience. If the audience is small enough, try to connect with each member of the audience. Otherwise, avoid looking down or reading notes. This will prove to your audience that you are prepared for your presentation.

Tip 2: Use movement. Consider analyzing the presentation space in advance and consider how you can use it to your advantage. You want to avoid pacing, but plan out some strategic movement. For example, when you transition to a new point think about moving to a new spot. Your audience may visualize or remember your points better. Remember, not all speeches or presentations have to be given from behind a podium!

Tip 3: Add in gestures for emphasis. If you have an interesting point that you want to highlight for your audience, use your hands to reference it. This also may help to keep the audience interested.

Tip 4: Dramatic pauses exist for a reason! Sometimes not saying anything at all can be a powerful nonverbal message. Build in dramatic pauses to add a serious note to a point or add weight to something important you want the audience to think about.

Tip 5: Vary your vocal delivery. Recall from above that how you speak is also considered nonverbal communication. Simply changing your volume, pace, or tone can add variety to your presentation while keeping your audience engaged.

Tip 6: Maintain a confident and positive facial expressions. You've probably heard the expression, "fake it until you make it." Be careful about what messages your face is sending the audience about your nerves. A smile or bright facial expression goes a long way in reassuring your audience that you've got this and are the expert in your topic.

Tip 7: Stand straight and have good posture. To appear the most confident in your presentations, stand straight an alert. Unfortunately for people who slouch or people with naturally poor posture, this may send an ambiguous message to your audience (i.e. a hunched over posture may insinuate that you are not confident in your presentation). A theatre professor once said, "think about having a penny between your shoulder blades. Keep your shoulders back to keep it from falling to the floor." This small mind trick may help you stand up straight.

Tip 8: Be mindful of your nervous "ticks." A lot of times when we get nervous during presentations we reflect this with nonverbal communication such as swaying, shifting weight from foot to foot, shaky hands, or gripping our notecards. Start paying attention to how your nerves manifest so you can work on avoiding them in the future. One way to do this is to start recording yourself presenting. You can then replay it and watch for these nervous behaviors.

Tip 9: Work on reducing your vocal fillers. No one likes to listen to a presentation where every other word is "like" or "uh." This implies to your audience that you are not only nervous, but also underprepared. Slow down and don't forget to breathe. These two easy steps often help reduce one's filler use. Again, record your practice speech and listen back to it for the use of fillers. Not everyone uses the same filler, but special attention should be paid to them.

Tip 10: Dress to impress! You wouldn't show up to a first date wearing a mustard stained pair of sweatpants (at least I hope you wouldn't) and you shouldn't wear them to a professional presentation either. Put more effort into your overall appearance on presentation day. It will not only boost your own confidence, but it will increase your credibility with the audience.

influence others' perception of an individual. Same thing with furniture, décor, and even lighting. Think of it as the space designed by a person can set the mood or tone for an encounter. Therefore, the physical layout or placement of things such as items in offices or even the location of the offices themselves can communicate a lot of information without requiring any verbal language.

Nonverbal Communication in a Digital World

Nonverbal communication is not just for in person communication. In 2020 when the COVID-19 pandemic forced college campuses to move online virtual classrooms. Professors everywhere suddenly had to navigate Zoom classes. Students would appear in virtual classes not wearing shirts or lying in bed eating while attending class. In fact, at one university in the Southeastern United States a male student attended a client meeting for a business class while shirtless on Zoom. This prompted a massive email to the entire college of business about students wearing inappropriate clothing while meeting clients. If you have a virtual meeting, presentation, or class keep in mind your nonverbal communication still matters. Your eye contact and gestures become even more important since the audience cannot see your entire body or movement. Also, simple things like posture and dressing appropriately can send signals that online meetings are just as important as in person ones.

Conclusion

The key takeaway from this chapter on nonverbal communication is to start paying attention to your own! Nonverbal communication happens all the time and we communicate more nonverbally than we do verbally. These are powerful messages, albeit open to many interpretations. Be open minded about these messages, especially when communicating with someone from a culture different than your own. Since there are many possible interpretations to nonverbal communication and it is different from one culture to another, be as unbiased and flexible as possible. Also, sometimes we send messages nonverbally that we may not intend to send. Keeping all of these things in mind may make you a better communicator.

Regarding your professional presentations, start focusing or monitoring your own nonverbal messages, particularly when you are nervous. We frequently move or act in ways we are not even aware of if we are anxious when speaking. However, learn to use your nonverbal communication to your advantage. Often, you can strategically plan nonverbal communication to add emphasis or highlight important pieces of information. Move around the presentation space with purpose and maintain eye contact with your audience. A strong posture and professional appearance will leave your audience with the impression that you are confident and prepared. As you gain more experience with public speaking, you should find yourself being more mindful and aware of your nonverbal communication. It takes time, but having confident and strong nonverbal communication while presenting really will make you a dynamic speaker!

7 Presentations

© Gorodenkoff/Shutterstock.com

"I have to give a PowerPoint at work on Monday." No, actually you have a presentation at work on Monday and a PowerPoint slide deck accompanies it. This chapter explores the different types of business presentations: sales pitch, group presentation, panel discussion, persuasive pitch, informative presentation or speech, and online situations. This chapter will only highlight the context of each presentation and where they may be encountered. Additional chapters will discuss organization, informative presentations, and persuasive speeches in depth.

Presentations come in all shapes and forms, and often we do not consider many of the "presentations" we make daily. Many students say, "I will never have to give a speech after this class," but often forget all the presentation scenarios they will face. Interview questions, self-introductions, elevator pitches, and requests for resources are all types of mini-presentations. This chapter explores common presentations in the professional context. Many students ask, "What's the difference between public speaking and business communication? Aren't these the same class, the same thing?" The answer is: context. Survey courses in public speaking are born from Aristotle and Socrates and the art of the skillful speaking and/or persuading. Business communication goes a step further to expand those principles and examine the contexts of business and organizations. It is this idea that guides the central concept for this chapter.

Professional Presentations

The first and arguably most important idea we believe is that professional presenting is NOT synonymous with boring presenting. Often, people who are untrained in business presenting take to the podium and read a bunch of facts to an audience, or take to the front of a room to read from PowerPoint slides. The truth is, like the principles of public speaking, business speaking needs to have power, emotion, energy, character, logic, charisma, dynamism, and great delivery. Essentially, the power of logos, pathos, and ethos needs to be found in business presenting too.

People buy products from those they like and trust.

Audiences trust people they find interesting, dynamic, and believable. If you simply read from PowerPoint slides, it does not look like you know your material. If you simply read numbers and facts from a script, it keeps you from being interesting. If you do not rehearse ahead of time, you will not be dynamic. Considering a habit typically forms after being performed for 10,000 hours; it suggests that a newer speaker needs as much rehearsal time as possible to have a shot at being good.

To set yourself apart from the competition, it is necessary to change your frame of mind on business presentations. They must not be boring; they must be energized and rehearsed. Your professional presentations need to tell a story regardless of what topic or context they attempt to convey. The next few parts of this chapter highlight common types of business presentations and ways to rethink the energy and dynamism that go into such a speech. Presentation structure is discussed in later chapters. Something we noticed over the pandemic is that the principles of effective business presentations are the same across traditional and technological platforms. Speakers, teachers, students, and partners need to rehearse, or at least run through, their materials. This is exclusive of the typical technological issues that seemingly plague all online meetings.

PowerPoint

Often college students are assigned a project in their courses and, either in a group or individually, they quip, "Who wants to do the PowerPoint, or What should go in the PowerPoint?" Shifting your focus on PowerPoint presenting needs to begin now. The presentation process begins with *content*. The content of any given project, presentation, report, or speech is what should dictate a visual tool like PowerPoint. Starting with the PowerPoint and working backward or creating a presentation inside a PowerPoint or Keynote program is going to waste a presenter's time and lead to a disjointed, often disorganized, presentation. So, the first order of business when considering a PowerPoint is the content. Is PowerPoint even needed or will handouts and pictures work? PowerPoint is no longer novel or dazzling, so just having one does not make your presentation any better than someone else's. The idea that a teacher expects it should not dictate whether you need it or not. In the business context, professionals create PowerPoint slides to tell a visual story, not because their boss said it was required.

© violetkaipa/Shutterstock.com

Considering that PowerPoint is no longer new or novel, let us go a step further and discuss how much audience members dislike presenters reading their slides word-for-word. Consider the time it takes to read aloud to a child, or when you have been read to as an audience member. Often, if there is a slide available then the audience member can read faster in her mind silently than a speaker can read from a slide. In other words: you need to stop reading to people. The same is true for making presentations over Zoom,

Teams, or other online programs. Reading slides to an audience located in various places, and at various times, makes for an arduous and tiresome presentation.

But how will I remember all the content? PowerPoint structure will be discussed later, but the bottom line is: your PowerPoint should not be your speaker notes in a visual outline. PowerPoint should be valid points needed to make a stronger case or a story for the audience to follow. You should build your own outline or notes separately from any visual presentation materials.

Sales Pitch

Thanks to the hit TV show *Shark Tank,* the word *pitch* became synonymous for persuasive presentation in the entrepreneurial world. The context dictates what you may call this persuasive presentation. To an end user, buyer, or client, a persuasive presentation may be called a sales pitch or a sales presentation. If you are presenting to an investor, stakeholder, or someone who manages the resources you seek, then you may call your presentation simply a pitch, or a product pitch. In both contexts, the end result is an "ask" where you as a speaker are requesting time, money, energy, or effort on behalf of the audience member. Ultimately persuasion, charisma, dynamics, and trust are important to convince audience members to move with you on your journey.

© iQoncept/Shutterstock.com

Pitches need to be well rehearsed, genuine, researched, and focused. If you are going to ask for anything as a speaker, you have to make sure you do your homework. It is good to know your audience, know your material, and be enthusiastic about your time in front of your potential client or investor. Remember the fundamental principles from PowerPoint, people will not give you things if they do not trust you; so make sure if you do a PowerPoint deck, you are not reading to a potential stakeholder.

Group Presentations

Business courses and business schools often require several group presentations. These go by several names: team presentations, group projects, case competitions, and pitch teams. The names may change, but the end goal is all the same — to give a beautiful, well-rehearsed multi-person presentation. Often, students are assigned group presentations with no direction on what to do, where to stand, how to organize the presentation, or the purpose of having three, four, or five people stand in front of the room. Structure and presenter placement are further discussed in chapter 15, but we will offer a few components of a beautiful group presentation now.

© holbox/Shutterstock.com

First, in the professional world, the purpose of people presenting in a team is typically functional. Each member of that presentation has a reason to be on that stage. This may change in a group Zoom meeting, where there is no "stage." In this case, each "presenter" should change their name in ways the rest of the meeting can see who is presenting. It may looking something like, "Chris — PRESENTER."

This allows for participants to message certain individuals, and/or expect who will be speaking. Perhaps one person worked on the finances of a project, while another worked on the marketing strategy. It may make sense that these people speak for different lengths of time and using different purposes for their time "on stage." So, the nuanced ways that group presentations are assigned in college may not lend itself to the way group presentations are used in the business world. More specifically, college students are sometimes forced into weird positions where a team has five people and everyone *must* speak for two minutes. This is odd as it lets delivery dictate content. Remember, it is the other way around — content should always dictate delivery.

Next, in the business world, the strongest speaker often is the person who knows the most about the material. Yet, in college sometimes there are excited speakers who have

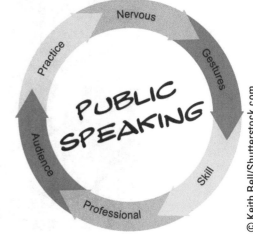

© Keith Bell/Shutterstock.com

not studied the purpose of their project. It is important for college groups to self-coach through skill level and knowledge of the material. Very few college group presentations are enjoyable and beneficial when presented by students who never practiced. We also heard from several students during the pandemic, that some group members felt it was not necessary to rehearse an online presentation, or conversely wanted to only meet via Zoom to rehearse an in-person presentation. Remember the channel. It's always important to rehearse a presenting in the manner in which you will be presenting. Zoom, practice on Zoom. In-person, practice in person.

It is so important to rehearse a group presentation as a whole team (and multiple times) in order to produce a beautiful presentation. Additionally, rehearsing eliminates nerves of the unknown. If you have a weaker speaker in your group, you can help him or her ahead of time rather than "hoping they don't make a mistake" on the day of the presentation. When untamed, nerves cause everyone to make mistakes — not just weaker speakers.

Sometimes college speakers perceive group presentations to be easier because they are not up front or on stage alone. The opposite is actually true. It takes more energy, effort, rehearsal, and collaboration to make a quality group presentation. Groups should acknowledge this when setting up their agenda for completing their project and the presentation. If a team is never available to meet, rehearse, or discuss a project virtually — then it should not be a team. Of course, college students have busy lives, so this is not always practical. However, working to overcome such challenges will set teams up for success.

Panel Discussions

Panel discussions are presentations that many students witness, but rarely ever participate in until after graduation. For this reason, we think it is important to discuss the synergy and rehearsal of a panel discussion and further explain the goal. Specifically, panels are a group of people assembled based on each individual speaker's areas of expertise. They are then invited to speak for a certain chunk of time on their specialty; often there is a moderator or question-and-answer period at the end of the formal presentation. We see this daily on press interviews with athletes, sane political and social commentary on television and on podcasts, and in academic and professional arenas like conferences and tradeshows.

Courtesy of Benjamin Videtto

Many times, the panelists will sit behind a table in the front of a room while a moderator transitions between speakers. If possible, stand and present during your time and engage the audiences just as you would any other speech. If you choose to sit, that does not mean you should read from your paper or notes. In an actual panel situation, you are asked to join based on your experience and expertise. You should still rehearse so you come across as practiced, knowledgeable, trustworthy, energetic, and sincere. Many untrained panel speakers miss this opportunity fraught with nerves that causes them to read from their notes. Do not let this happen to you!

One thing to consider when participating in a panel discussion online is, how do you fit into the lineup? Make sure to ask your host what the goals are with having you join the conversation. How much time do you have? How similar or different are you to the other panelists? During the last couple of years your authors participated as guests in various panels. Sometimes fellow panelists had not practiced or outlined their remarks and would veer completely out of the time constraints. Other times the synergy of the panelists was magical. Understanding the dynamics of a panel discussion, as well as your individual responsibility while serving on a panel, creates a solid group presentation.

Informative Presentations and Reports

Informative presentations assume two things about the contextual desires of the audience—they want to be there and/or they are interested in the content you are about to present. Even if your informative presentation is a report at the beginning of every week or every work shift, it should be presented in a "so what?" format. Why is this information important to the people who have come to here? Show them relevance and relatability.

Many informative presentations and reports use a lot of numbers and facts. It is true facts and numbers show importance and often tell a story of why something is the way it is. However, audience members remember roughly 12% of what they hear and about 20% of what they see and hear. So, as a presenter, it is your responsibility to really tie the known with the unknown, so listeners will actually remember what you say. It is your job to then use visuals, if necessary, and tell the story of why this information is relevant.

Reports do not have to be boring. If you are presenting a report, it is time to throw out the elementary school thought that all reports are boring book reviews. Sure, not all accounting and finance information is exciting, but it could be to your invited and attending audience members. For example, you could make

© PORTRAIT IMAGES ASIA BY NONWARIT/
Shutterstock.com

a statement like, "Our company made $20,000 in profit this quarter," and leave it at that. Or, you could say it this way, "Our company made $20,000 in profit this quarter which is twice as much as this time last year and four times as much as two years ago. This puts us on track for continued growth and the addition of another employee." Now, we can see the company is doing well and this is exciting! Not every statement has to be justified this way, but those "so what?" moments need to be included in your speech or you will leave your audience confused, complacent, and bored.

Online Speaking

Facetime, Skype, WebX, Go to Meeting — no matter the name of the software, the time is here when you will present to an online audience. Many students have requested coaching for Zoom interviews — and rightfully so! It is a very odd feeling to not be able to read your audience in real time or see them at all in some cases. Now we can add Zoom, Teams, and Google hangouts and Google classrooms to this list. Skype was purchased by Microsoft and folded into Teams, and as technology booms we can assume more mergers and acquisitions will take place in the tech space. What follows still remains. The principles of good presenting never go out of style.

The first order of business with online presenting are the exact same principles mentioned before. It pays to be organized and rehearsed. Rehearsing online presentations for interviews and speeches allows you to become more familiar with the software and ultimately the sound of your own voice. Many of us dislike how we sound when recorded, so if you are tasked with uploading a prerecorded presentation of yourself, make sure you start early and run the presentation a few times. Unless you are fearless or familiar with this medium, you will probably not like the way you sound on the first recording.

During an online presentation or interview, it is important to be rehearsed and loud. Hardware has gotten good, but it is essential to make sure you have a working microphone and are located in a quiet room with good lighting. Also, be aware of what is in the background of your camera shot. You do not want to reveal too many personal details about who you are (we will discuss this concept further). You want to be the focus of the presentation and not have items that distract your audience such as lots of different furniture, books, kids' toys, pets, etc. in the background. It can become a game of 'seek and find' for the audience and not listening to your information.

© Andrey_Popov/Shutterstock.com

Dressing professionally is imperative as well. Remember the mass communication format of online presenting and video removes a lot of real-time feedback, which in many cases removes a lot of an individual's natural charm. Dress the part for the presentation. Just because we cannot fully see your body in a webcast does not mean you are able to wear pajama bottoms. You want to feel the same pressure of presentations, as if you were live. Practicing and looking good are the main concepts to consider about online presenting.

Additionally, if you have been given feedback that you need more vocal inflection or variety, it is time to work on getting rid of fillers and that monotone talk. Sure, this is true for all presentations, but if you tend to use many fillers like "uh" or "like," this will be heightened when you present online. Often times, listeners turn on recorded presentations simply to listen. It is imperative to make sure your vocal delivery is top quality.

In this chapter, we mentioned several contexts for business presenting. Our goal is to help set students apart from the competition and aid them in working to become interesting, dynamic, professional presenters. The main thing to remember is that business presentations do not equate to boring presentations. It is a good speaker's job to make sure she engages her audience, does her homework, starts early, tells a story, and relates the "so what?" to the audience. The situations mentioned above all have potential to be engaging, interesting, and dynamic. It is up to the speaker to work to convey the importance and interesting aspect of his or her presentation.

Chapter

8 Organization and Structure

So, you have to give a presentation and already selected your topic; now, how in the world do you organization all of your thoughts, ideas, and research? This chapter opens with a discussion of structure, as it relates to speaking. In order to effectively articulate the purpose of your presentation, you will need to strategize how to set it up. This chapter will walk you through the most common and useful organizational patterns of the speaking world. There are lots of different styles out there, but for the purposes of public business communication presentations, we are going to introduce you (or re-introduce you) to the five main options: topical, chronological, spatial, problem-solution, and cause-effect. We will also discuss presentation introductions and conclusions.

© Rawpixel.com/Shutterstock.com

Topical Organizational Format

We will use the terms "structure" and "format" and "pattern" interchangeably for a more engaging discussion. Many beginning speakers have not been trained (yet) on this invaluable tool of public presentation. Some speakers think speeches and presentations are one big manuscript or story; others use an English class essay format, which in some cases may work but requires adjustments for an oral delivery. We want to educate you on these efficient ways to create structure, so your audience can follow your message and you can better memorize/remember your presentation.

Topical formatting, as the name indicates, organizes subtopics in a way that supports larger main ideas all with the purpose of supporting the thesis.

The thesis is the main idea and encompasses the purpose of the presentation. The "topic" of the talk is housed within the thesis statement.

Let us look at Business School Applications presented visually:

Thesis: Navigating MBA and graduate school applications can be confusing; this talk simplifies the process!

Main points:

  A. Necessary Entry Exams/working through barriers
  B. The purpose of an MBA
  C. Tips for fees and value

All of these main points work to support the thesis that sometimes the graduate school process is confusing, and the points work to help the listeners navigate the landscape of applying for the MBA. We call these *topics*; hence—the topical organizational pattern. Each of these main points/topics will eventually have subtopics that support that particular point.

Visually:

  A. Necessary Entry Exams/Working Through Barriers
    1. MBA students take the GMAT
    2. Accounting and marketing students can take the GMAT or the GRE
    3. Types of GPAs
    4. Any major can do a master's in business
  B. The Purpose of the MBA
    1. Career advancement
    2. Learn more skills
    3. Earn more money at current career
    4. What an MBA doesn't do
  C. Tips for Fees and Value
    1. Employers typically don't care about prestige
    2. Avoid for-profit schools
    3. State schools are usually cheaper
    4. Online programs can be expensive, so be careful
    5. Assistantships save money and help with costs

Essentially, we begin to build-out an outline with which many students are familiar. Structure. Structure. Structure. We cannot emphasize this enough. Structure like this gives shape to an oral presentation that often could lose listeners in the middle. Speakers should add transitions between main points and walk listeners through the journey of the presentation. Remember the audience will not have your outline so you have to verbally indicate when you are moving from one topic to the next!

Why it is great: The Topical Format is excellent because it can be arranged in ways the author/speaker finds the most logical. Deciding how to organize your main points breaks down into three different options: primacy, recency, and complexity. **Primacy** means that you start with your strongest main point first. Maybe you believe it will really grab your audience to pay attention right off the bat. In the example above, perhaps a speaker wishes to put point B: the purpose of an MBA first instead of the middle. This works. Topical formatting allows the speaker to do this. **Recency** is the exact opposite; the strongest point goes last in the organization. Some audience members might remember the last thing that is presented the best, or the item that was most "recently" discussed. So, back to our example, maybe point B should be the clincher at the end of the presentation. The last option, **complexity**, is all about the progression or difficulty of information. You want to ease your audience into your presentation with data they can understand and then start rolling toward the more "complex" information. Think about a basic algebra course. The instructors should not start week one with formulas like $s = ut + \frac{1}{2} at \sqrt{540}$. Students would be submitting drop slips really quickly! Instead you start with some basics everyone can grasp $x + 2 = 6$. Once you have the audience, then you can progress with harder information.

In addition, the topical organization helps with larger presentations. Many speeches and talks in business contexts are 10 minutes to an hour long and sometimes with multiple presenters. This format allows for the creation of "sections" to keep both the presenters and the audience on track. For 10 minutes, ensure that each topic has about 3 minutes of explanation (allowing time for an intro and conclusion). For a multi-person presentation, each individual prepares to speak on one main point and transitions move the speech from person to person.

Chronological Organizational Format

The **Chronological** pattern is pretty common to many speakers, yet often forgotten about when creating a presentation. As the title infers, the strategy here is ordinal.

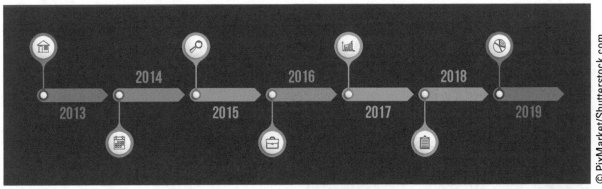

© PixMarket/Shutterstock.com

These presentations work well in telling a story through time or when giving directions. Often presenters jump around or do not choose this pattern, when it would have been a better choice. Let us take the MBA topic again, but put it in a more perfunctory sense and slot it into the Chronological Organizational Format.

Thesis: Navigating MBA and graduate school applications can be confusing; this step-by-step talk simplifies that!

    A. Important Deadlines
        1. GMAT exams offered
        2. College admission deadlines
        3. Days deposits are typically due
        4. The FAFSA form
    B. Before you are accepted
        1. Decide if you want to work online or drive to campus
        2. Decide the value you want to place into your MBA experience
        3. Contact admission specialists to inquire about your status
    C. Once you are accepted
        1. Financing your education
        2. How much to work
        3. What the MBA will do for you

Sure, this looks a little like the Topical Format, but if you did this particular outline in a different order, it would look funny. The same is true for historical presentations of people or data. Discussing US Presidents historically out of order would be a bit odd. If you changed the thesis to *US Presidents with the Fewest Number of Scandals*, this by default falls to the Topical pattern and you head each main idea with a president.

Speakers who find themselves in training, teaching, HR, and other explanatory contexts will begin to analyze and see the benefits of using the Chronological pattern. As with Topical, you should build out an outline with subpoints and transitions to complete the speaking outline for your presentation.

We cannot stress enough the importance of structure when preparing and presenting a presentation. And, remember what we discussed before—you are not "writing a PowerPoint" as your speech. You should create the structural outline first. Then, if you need a PowerPoint to help display your information, it is then that you create a PowerPoint that accompanies your outline, not the other way around.

Spatial Organizational Format

Just like with chronological, it is all in the name. The **Spatial** format refers to "space" and the information is organized in relation to one another. Spatial works really well, if you need to do a presentation that

© Rawpixel.com/Shutterstock.com

involves physical locations or geography, and it can also work in conjunction with chronological. Think about preparing a presentation as a tour guide for a major city like New York.

There is no way you could cover every point of history on an hour-long tour, and you have to consider which locations are closer together to make the most of your time. That is a spatial approach. It is all about the layout, physical structure, and/or direction you need the audience to follow.

Problem–Solution Organizational Format

The next two organizational options are similar in nature. Both could work for an informative or persuasive presentation, as it is all about your speaking goal.

With the **problem–solution** format, the speaker presents the different problems occurring because of a specific event and then goes into detail about the solution(s) available. With an informative presentation, you would not "persuade" or tell the audience what to do—you are just providing the information on the different solution options, whereas a persuasive presentation would call the audience to act and take part in one of the solutions to the problem.

Cause–Effect Organizational Format

The last organizational option is the **cause–effect** format which, like the problem–solution, breaks down into the speaker presenting different causes or issues and the effects taking place. A sample topic could be what caused the increased number of obese people in the United States over the last 10 years, and how it has affected health rates. Once again, the first step the speaker needs to determine is the goal of the message. Are you simply providing the facts/figures (informative) or are you going to convince your audience (persuade) to act?

The organizational formats presented are the most common ones used in presentations; however, this does not mean other options are not available. The important items to consider include your topic, your goal as a presenter, and to have a clear format for the audience to follow.

Introductions

There's an old cliché that goes, "You never have a second chance to make a first impression." This is also true when you approach the front of the room/stage/table to make your presentation. You may have made a personal impression on those with whom you were sitting with or with your colleagues; or you worked the room beforehand and made a connection with the crowd. However, the first 30 seconds and the overall opening of your time upfront has to be magnetic or you will lose your audience immediately—once they are gone, it is very difficult to convince the audience they need to listen.

First, let us discuss the structure of the **introduction**. There are four major components to every presentation introduction. These include: attention-getter (hook), thesis, preview, and credibility (why are you up front/why are you tied to this topic/what do you care and why should they?). These can manifest in any order, but the attention-getter is absolutely and always first. Not your name. Not your topic. Not your excuses for being unprepared or a comment about the weather—but the attention-getter goes first.

Continuing with the MBA presentation, here's a sample introduction:

> US News and World Report said in its May 2017 edition that employees with master's degrees on average earn one million dollars more over a lifetime than their colleagues with a bachelor's degree (need citation). What would you do with a million dollars? House? Trip? Donate it? For many of us it's paying back these student loans. It's becoming more apparent that MBAs are the way to go for business students and today we are going to navigate the MBA and graduate school applications which can be confusing; in order to simplify the process on the way to that one million dollars. My name is Steve Smith, and I'm not actually about the money—this is something I've wanted to do for a while now in order to start my own business. I want to share with you how to work through barriers, the purpose of the MBA, and ways to mitigate fees.

This example has the attention-getter first followed by the thesis, credibility, and main points. Let us look at it broken down into an outline format:

> **Attention Getter**: US News and World Report said in its May 2017 edition that employees with master's degrees on average earn one million dollars more over a lifetime than their colleagues with a bachelor's degree (need citation). What would you do with a million dollars? House? Trip? Donate it? For many of us it's paying back those student loans.

> **Thesis:** It's becoming more apparent that MBAs are the way to go for business students and today we are going to navigate the MBA and graduate school applications which can be confusing; in order to simplify the process on the way to that one million dollars.
>
> **Credibility:** My name is Steve Smith, and I'm not actually about the money—this is something I've wanted to do for a while now in order to start my own business.
>
> **Preview of Main Points:** I want to share with you how to work through barriers, the purpose of the MBA, and ways to mitigate fees.

The final step is a solid transition that moves listeners into the first main point. The goal is to make the flow of the speech beautiful and articulate and not choppy.

There are many types of hooks to use as an **attention-getter**: facts/quotes, statistics, examples and stories, humor (be careful not to offend your audience), visuals (usually highlighting one of the other types: stats/facts/stories), and questions. Let us discuss questions for a minute.

When using a question as an opening attention-getter, make sure you think very carefully about the purpose of the question and what you are trying to do with the reaction the audience gives to the question. Many people agree there are two main types of questions: 1) Rhetorical for which no answer is expected. For example, "Can you believe it's so cold outside again?" and 2) Real questions, for which you are polling the audience. For example, "How many people in here like money?"

Let us be clear! Neither of these questions are exciting, fresh, attention-grabbing, fun, or witty. Yet, this is how so many classroom presentations begin. "Who likes money? So I'm going to tell you about the MBA." This is terribly boring.

First, who does not like money? But second, what about those three volunteer-minded people in class who in-effect, are not actually driven by money—they now dislike you. So, most of the room finds you boring and three of your colleagues think you are greedy. Nice work.

To set themselves apart, speakers need to think clearly why they choose the attention-getters they do. Simple questions as an "opener" may have been fine in middle school, but now the stakes have changed and so too should the speech techniques.

© Constantin Stanciu/Shutterstock.com

How to do this? Be creative. If you are presenting to a client, tell them what one million dollars could do for their business. If speaking with colleagues, do an audience analysis to know what they like and do not like. People love to hear about themselves—trust us. The bottom line here is an attention-getter should gain attention and not make the crowd believe that you will bore them to tears. It's time to step-it-up and present like you mean it! It starts with the first thirty seconds.

The other step in the Introduction we need to discuss concerns your **credibility**. What makes YOU a good person to speak on this topic?

So, let us discuss some ways you can show your audience you are a trustworthy person capable of speaking on the subject. First, do you have any specific education on the subject matter? Think about degrees, licenses, or certificates you may have that apply to the situation. Even if you do not have specific credentials, you may have expertise on the matter because it is something you deal with personally or on an everyday basis. Next, what kind of passion or enthusiasm do you have about the topic? Remember you want to select a topic you are interested in, that you care about, or maybe it is something that gets you angry and fired up. That passion is evident when delivering a message on a topic that captures your interest. Finally,

© paseven/Shutterstock.com

we have discussed perception and our initial first impressions of people. Remember that your appearance can also impact your credibility. Did you come dressed to impress or just rolled out of bed? Also, think how your appearance can enhance or take away from your message. Are there certain uniforms or equipment that would be present in the situation you are discussing? Think about scrubs, chef jackets, military uniforms, etc. as examples to go along with speech content. On the flip side, you do not want your appearance to distract or take away credibility with your message. For example, you do not want to give a speech _against_ legalizing marijuana and be wearing a shirt with this on it:

Credibility works two ways; you can have credibility as a speaker (because of your background, training, etc.), but you also have to earn credibility from your audience. Just because you have specific degrees in the field does not mean you can communicate the information clearly to your audience. (How many professors have you had that are brilliant minds in their field, but cannot explain the concepts clearly in an introductory class?) Avoid credibility statements like, "I have researched this topic for two weeks and feel qualified to speak to you." Every presenter "should" research their topic before a speech. That does not connect you to the topic or make you more qualified than the next person. If you feel you do not have any credibility or connection to your subject you may want to rethink your topic selection.

Conclusions

Conclusions recap and summarize what the entire presentation was about. They seek to remind, end memorably, and provide psychological closure to the audience. We call the mechanics of this "RE3." This refers to the first two letters of the THREE things you must do in a conclusion. You must 1) Restate the thesis, 2) Review the preview, and 3) Revisit the attention-getter with your final thought. Essentially, you are driving home the point, reminding the audience where they have been, and closing in a way that is memorable. For example:

> Today we've discussed the journey to the MBA and navigating the somewhat confusing process. We discussed important dates and tests; took a walk through the importance and purpose of the MBA; and evaluated a few ways to save some money after accepting a school's offer. I know that many will earn one million dollars over the course of their working lives. For me, I hope to open my business the T-shirt shack and earn my cool million that way. I hope you'll come by for that floral tourist shirt you always wanted!

The listener is reminded of the entire last 10 or so minutes and brought back to the opening attention-getter of the one million dollars. They are reminded that the speaker is doing the same process (not always necessary, but helpful), and left with a memorable image of a T-shirt shack selling floral printed shirts out on the beach. This conclusion is better than saying, "That's it!"

So many speakers do not have a plan for the conclusion of their presentations. In fact, this is one of the most important parts of the presentation because it has the opportunity to leave a memorable mark on your audience. You want the conclusion, like the rest of the presentation, to look rehearsed, polished, and fresh. What you do not want it to look like is someone who is so ready to be done that you rush through the last thirty seconds to get off the stage. No.

© stoatphoto/Shutterstock.com

The other thing many speakers do is: like a robot they say, "Any questions?" Not in a professional or practical way, but in a culturally scripted pointless way. First, make sure you are able to take questions immediately following your presentation. If it is a panel discussion, the order may be for each person to present and then for the entire room to ask questions of everyone at the same time. Second, it is about the delivery of opening up the floor to your audience. Many speakers are not even finished with their last real sentence before in the same speed and tone they roll into "Any questions?" End your presentation, wait for applause, then open for questions. If people do not have questions, does that mean you were thorough, or boring? Are you prepared to answer questions?

Instead, if there is time, say something more personable like, "So, our journey was a deep one, what questions do you have for me?" If no one asks anything say something professional like, "If you think of something later, or I see you at lunch please don't hesitate to make contact and/or ask. Thank you so much." This may actually get you another round of applause—if you want it.

The most important thing to do when concluding a presentation is to end memorably. "Any questions" isn't memorable—it's boring. (The same goes for, ". . . and these are my references" - do not make that your closing statement!) Maya Angelou told us, "People will forget what you said, forget what you did, but they will always remember the way you made them feel." A good speech does this!

Transitions

One final element to discuss are the transitions. Unfortunately, most speakers forget to include them during a speech, thinking it is clear how you have organized the presentation. Keep in mind that, although you have researched, prepared, and practiced your information for the speech, this is the first time your audience is hearing the content. They need clear direction as much as organization in a speech.

© iQoncept/Shutterstock.com

The point of including **transitions** is to notify your audience as you move from one section of your speech into the next, and transitions can be both verbal and nonverbal. So, let us examine an example of a transitions with our MBA topic:

A. Important Deadlines
   1. GMAT exams offered
   2. College admission deadlines
   3. Days deposits are typically due
   4. The FAFSA form

Transition: Now that we have examined deadlines and when to submit forms, let's talk about steps you need to select the best program for you.

B. Before you are accepted
   1. Decide if you want to work online or drive to campus
   2. Decide the value you want to place into your MBA experience
   3. Contact admission specialists to inquire about your status

You see the transition takes the audience from one point to the next. Think of transitions as road signs to let people know where you are going with the information. In addition, you can literally "move" around the room as you move between points in your speech. Some speakers are taught the Triangle Method when practicing calculated movement in their presentations. The goal is to walk the space and create a 'triangle' shape with your walking path.

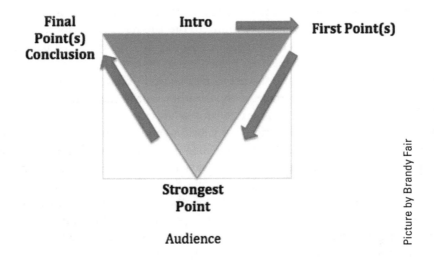

Picture by Brandy Fair

We mapped out one example of a Triangle Method presentation for you to see an option for moving around during a speech. You start square with your audience, move to one side as you go into the body, come up close as you hit the really passionate moment in your speech, and then back away to conclude. The one thing to keep in mind is that if you are not comfortable moving then nonverbal transitions may not be the best approach for you. You are not required to move if it makes you more nervous or throws off your delivery. Remember verbal transitions are much more important for the audience to clearly follow along.

To this point, we have discussed organizational patterns for speaking including Topical, Chronological Format, Spatial, Problem–Solution, and Cause–Effect. We also touched on introductions and conclusions and their importance in grabbing the audience's attention immediately and leaving with something they remember long after you are finished.

© Colored Lights/Shutterstock.com

Although speaking is not necessarily easy, it can be fun, rewarding, and professional, if done correctly. Structure is the most important thing when beginning to prepare remarks on most subjects. Make sure to know your purpose and thesis and go from there in selecting an organizational pattern and outlining your presentation. Do not be fooled that business presentations do not have "academic style" thesis statements. "To share with the stakeholders the success of this quarter's report," is absolutely a thesis. Many times, thesis statements are not clearly verbalized thus, leading us to believe there is not one—but there is always a goal. Writing it down is the beginning to successful structure.

Beyond structure, we discussed introductions, conclusions, and transitions. Three very important aspects of a presentation often overlooked. We strongly encourage you to avoid simple pointless questions and move to deeper, more creative, more professional ways to begin a presentation. Finally, conclusions leave a mark on an audience. Saying, "That's it—any questions?," is probably the fastest way to get to lunch, but it is also the fastest way to be forgotten. Remember to RE3 and end memorably. Included is a sample outline to reference to see how a fully prepared speech outline looks. It is not just key ideas or bullet points (those are great to prepare presentation notes), but instead a fully laid-out, "perfect world" plan of what you want to say during your speech. Hopefully, the chapter provided guidance on how to organize any type of presentation you need to make in school or at work.

Chapter

9 Informative Communication

As we mentioned earlier in the text, different types of presentations have different goals which alter the context in which the presentation will be given. Beginning speakers are usually happily surprised to learn this and eager to change some of their strategies in order to better meet the needs of audience members. Persuasive speakers' audiences can be a mix of people with many different motivations and reasons for listening to a presenter. Some may come because they are hostile and "demand answers." Others may be there as an invitee, but who are not willing yet to part with their own beliefs. There are multiple reasons.

The good news about informative speaking is the crowd is typically less obtuse than in the persuasive event. In everyday life, we encounter informative speaking at museums, aquariums, parks, schools; places we have chosen to go or where we seek knowledge or information. In the business and organizational world, informative speaking typically finds itself in two situations: mandatory and voluntary. In both situations, we can assume that the information is important for and to someone since an effort is being made for the public transfer of knowledge. Speakers who are presenting at a mandatory informative briefing event have their work cut out for them to be dynamic, interested, interesting, charismatic, likable, and earnest. Speakers who have a voluntary audience before them have the same set of responsibilities, but perhaps not with as much pressure since people chose to hear the presentation. Bottom line: people need to know and understand what you are telling them. Enter informative speaking strategy.

The root of an **informative presentation** is all about the "inform" word. (Mind-blowing we know!) As a speaker, your goal is to share new information with your audience to create a new or enhanced understanding of the subject matter presented. Keep in mind the word *new* in the definition. Unfortunately, many beginning speakers select informative topics they are comfortable with and do not consider their audience members. If the audience is already familiar with your content, then you give them permission to not pay attention or engage.

© Zerbor/Shutterstock.com

Types of Informative Presentations

Thousands of options exist when selecting an informative topic. In a business setting, your topic may be assigned based on what information the audience needs (e.g., new procedures). However, you may have the opportunity to select your own subject matter, which can be overwhelming with the variety of choices that exist. Here are some different categories to think about when deciding on your topic.

Object—anything you can see or touch. Think about a speech about a specific location, monuments, animals, gadgets, etc.

Procedure—the "how to" speech. Some examples include applying for financial aid, how to 'ace' an interview, the process to hire a new employee, etc.

Person(s)—about an individual or group of people. This could include anyone dead or alive from celebrities, to serial killers, politicians, comedians, astronauts, you name it.

Events—a historical moment or upcoming occasion. Describing the events leading up to the bombing of Pearl Harbor, the Great Chicago Fire, hosting a benefit for your workplace, etc.

Ideas—new or innovative concepts. With an Idea topic, you have to be careful to remain neutral during your speech. A good approach would be to present both sides (pro/con) on the issue. (Remember this is an informative speech, not persuasive, so your job is to only present the material). Examples might include the legalization of marijuana, GMOs in food, cloning and stem cell research, etc.

Make Your Presentation Clear

Remember the goal of informative speaking: to introduce *new* information to your audience. Since the content is relatively new to your receivers, it is important to plan steps to assist them in grasping the content. You do not want your audience to leave you presentation more confused than before you started! Here are some items to keep in mind as you plan and prepare.

Keep Ideas Simple—Just because you are presenting new concepts does not mean that you have to use fancy language and jargon. That will turn off your audience members quickly! We will discuss this idea further in the chapter concerning listening. It will be necessary for you to break down information, so your audience understands your presentation. Define new terms, show images, or even ask your audience during your speech if they understand your information.

Make **Comparisons**—A good way to explain new terms or concepts is to compare them to something the audience is already familiar with. Think about trying to teach someone how to play piano. You might compare familiarizing yourself with the piano keys to typing on a computer. Think about how quickly you can complete work when you do not have to look down at what letters to press. The same concept applies for playing the piano. It is easier to move across the keyboard when you do not have to look down to see if you are pressing the correct key. If possible, ask the audience for comparison examples as well. An engaged, interactive audience can create further understanding of the concepts.

Be **Selective about Content**—There is no way to cover "everything" about an event in history, a person's life, etc. in one informative speech. How much time have you been allotted for your presentation? That could really narrow down what you can discuss. The solution is not, "I'll just talk fast so I can cover more information." Remember, this is new information for your audience, so speeding up will not allow time to absorb or retain the information. You will have to pick and choose what information you believe is pertinent enough to include in your presentation, and then keep a reasonable pace when presenting so the audience can grab onto the content.

Keep It Interesting

Regardless if your audience chose to listen or was required to attend, your presentation needs to be interesting. It is terrible to sit through a presentation where even the speaker seems bored with the information. Just because we are "forced" to be present does not mean you can relax with the preparation of your information.

© Rawpixel.com/Shutterstock.com

First, try to relate to your audience, if possible. Knowing audience members prior to a presentation can be both a blessing and a curse. It is a blessing to have a sense of familiarity with the individuals and already know what previous information has been presented within the organization. However, a familiar audience can serve to be a tougher crowd because they know you and will see you again after your session is complete. A single presentation can forever change how your coworkers view you after it is completed. Were you knowledgeable, prepared and someone they would gladly listen to in the future, or were you scattered, monotone, and never called upon to present again? An unfamiliar audience can be difficult as well because you have no prior knowledge of who they are, why they attend (by choice or force), and what they already know about the subject matter. As a speaker, you might see if you can survey your audience prior to the presentation to learn their current knowledge on your topic. If your goal is to teach new technology, you might find out if it will be a room full of beginners, do they have some experience, or need advanced directives to improve performance? Each level of knowledge could be a completely different presentation for you to prepare.

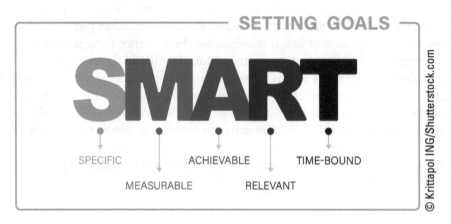

Define a specific **goal** for your presentation. Make your goals SMART ones too - Specific, Measurable, Achievable, Relevant, Time-Bound. You know what you want to present, but let your audience in on your objectives too. By announcing your expectations right up front, the listeners have a clear roadmap of what information you plan to cover, the different aspects, and what you want the audience to walk away knowing. Informative presentations (especially to a contained audience) need to be clear and concise versus an abstract approach to new concepts. Short, sweet, and to the point will help gain the audience's favor.

Have fun with it! This may require a lot of performance on your part as the presenter, especially if it is "boring" information about new policies and procedures. We do not always get to choose the topics we present, but we do have the choice in "how" we execute the information. If your delivery is flat, monotone, and you simply go through the motions in front of the audience, then why should they care? You might feel like a phony by presenting upbeat and positive but if it helps your audience retain the information, you have done your job (very similar to teaching).

Bring in aids to assist. We will talk about presentation aids in depth in a later chapter, but using additional materials can keep an audience focused instead of you speaking the entire time. Include videos, provide handouts, use pictures, or whatever you need to help make your concepts clear. Refer to the Visuals chapter for specific guidelines and suggestions about incorporating aids effectively into a speech.

Help Audience Retain Information

There are two types of presentations we often remember for a long time: the really good or the really bad. How do you want your speech described when it is all said and done? Granted not everyone will love everything you prepare, but there are a few steps to help your audience retain information (in a positive way) after the speech has concluded.

Redundancy

Tell them what you're going to tell them, Tell them, Tell them what you told them. This is a common phrase when it comes to speech writing and organization. You experienced it firsthand as you read through the content about organization and structure. Although redundancy sounds like a bad thing, when it comes to public speaking, it helps the message "stick" with your audience. Most people do not learn and retain information

by just hearing something one time. However, when you repeat a set of facts over and over, the audience members are more likely to leave your presentation remembering the important points in your speech. Think about the structure of your outline. In the introduction, you preview your main points. The body covers the main points in-depth. Finally, the conclusion includes a review of your main points. See the repetition? If nothing else, your audience will hopefully remember the key ideas you covered.

Presenting to Adults

Typically, your audience will be a room full of adults, whether it takes place in a classroom of your peers or within the workplace. Adults have certain expectations when it comes to presentations versus how you would prepare a presentation for children. Several researchers (Galbraith & Fouch, 2007; Kennedy, 2003; Palis & Quiros, 2014) examined different learning principles when preparing information for an adult audience.

First and foremost, you have to convince your audience about their need to learn something right at the beginning of your speech (Palis & Quiros, 2014). This coincides with the goal of your presentation. Although an informative speech, you may have to "persuade" your audience members about the need to listen and pay attention to the information. Why is the information relevant to them? How will it help in their everyday lives? What will they gain after listening to your content? Be sure to make the connection between the topic and your audience.

Second, realize an adult audience comes to the situation with prior knowledge, experience, and opinions (sometimes strong ones) about your topic. Galbraith and Fouch (2007) highlight that previous experiences should be incorporated into the presentation versus ignored as it may feel as if the presenter is belittling their audience. They go on to discuss how an audience member's "baggage" illustrates how life experience can serve as a barrier or a positive asset in an informative session. Barriers can include the "we tried this in the past," "why do we have to change," or "what can you teach me? I've been on the job longer than you've been alive," type mentalities. Yes, these are potential issues of some audience members you will face. Hopefully you can find a way to turn the barriers into benefits instead. Incorporate individuals' experiences, let them express what worked/did not work in the past, and include their examples as you present. Acknowledging their experience is always better than trying to silence or ignore their feelings.

Finally, keep in mind an adult audience's expectations and retention levels when it comes to new information. Kennedy (2003) discussed how an adult audience expects to use the information presented immediately on the job. They perceive that the speaker was scheduled at a specific day/time because of the nature of the information. "The reason we are discussing a new procedure is because it will go into effect next week" is an example of the mindset. If the information was not pertinent or timely, then there is not a need to review new concepts now. In addition, Kennedy (2003) emphasized that adults' retention levels decline with age, so it is important to use the information regularly in their jobs in order to maintain their level of knowledge. Preparing two presentations may be the best approach if the training is not immediately necessary: speech #1 to introduce change is coming and provide a summary overview, and then speech #2 when it is time to start learning how to use the new process.

Social Media and Other Outlets

As time progresses, we must acknowledge other ways informative communication takes place in the business context. Remember when someone looks at your LinkedIn profile and videos, personal social media, blogs, Tweets, and other mass media platforms, you are projecting an informative communicative image. This is your brand. You want to make sure you are communicating exactly what you mean the best way possible. Message meanings lie with the receiver of those messages. In a public format like a presentation or speech, someone can ask a question for clarity. If you have a YouTube channel, Instagram, TikTok, or other professional media outlet, the potential for someone to make his or her own assumptions about your brand is much greater. Make sure to edit and evaluate your personal and professional brands regularly.

Additionally, emails, memos, minutes, reports, and visual presentations all fall within informative speaking. Be sure to review (or have someone edit) all of these collateral materials. Misspellings and misunderstandings will cause someone to potentially misinterpret what it is you are trying to convey. This could result in losing business, deals, or a job. Informative communication is everywhere!

Finally, informative communication in social media allows for misunderstandings and unintended messages. Make sure you "clean up" your personal and professional brands by editing your materials and asking someone you trust to look at your materials. Seeing things from someone else's perspective may help close a deal or gain a client.

TED Talks

People love TED Talks. You would be hard-pressed to find someone who has something negative to say about *all* TEDTalks. In general, they are pretty interesting and dynamic. Sometimes, faculty members use TedTalks in classes to aid with their teaching material. Other times, friends send each other links to the TED Talks they've seen because they would like to share. In fact, TED's slogan is "ideas worth sharing."

TED talks are every bit the epitome of informative speaking. Experts, storytellers, ideas people, teachers, scientists, and more come to the TED world stage to give a speech about an idea. What makes these talks intriguing is regardless of how close the topic is to something we are personally associated, we can relate or understand the thesis and idea. *This* is the beauty of TED talks. It is this premise newer speakers should seek to embrace—try every avenue to relate to your audience regardless of their current understanding of your topic.

Some of the most popular TED talks of all time are:

1. **Sir Ken Robinson**, Do Schools Kill Creativity? (2006), 72 million views
2. **Amy Cuddy**, How Body Language May Shape Who You Are (2012), 64 million views
3. **Simon Sinek**, How Great Leaders Inspire Action (2009), 57 million views
4. **Brene' Brown**, The Power of Vulnerability (2010), 56 million views
5. **Tim Urban**, Inside the Mind of a Master Procrastinator (2016), 59 million views

May applaud how diverse the complete list is with topics of all kinds. Time permitting you should take a look at these short speeches. While viewing, you will find many of the elements from this chapter such as the ability to compel the adult audience in the beginning, telling the audience why this topic is important to the speaker and subsequently the audience, and how a dynamic performance can make a previously unaware audience member engaged.

Carmine Gallo published a book *Talk Like TED* where he analyzed hours of footage of the most popular TED talks in search of common threads that make the speeches dynamic. One of the most important findings was *passion*. Using the research analytics he created, it was evident that passionate delivery, as well as narrative anecdotes, were the reasons the most popular talks were so captivating. Stories compelled viewers to identify with the speaker and connect to their material. As an informative speaker, you can take these different tactics and begin to apply them to your own speaking.

Many beginning speakers ask us, "Is it OK to tell a short story?" Yes! Please do—yes, yes, yes! Of course, it is important to make sure it is valid and the audience understands the purpose. However, we have found that too few people in daily professional speaking tell stories. These stories need not always be personal, they can be about an article you read or a story you heard in class or at work. Remember some of the purposes of storytelling: lesson learned, rags to riches, underdog as the hero. Sometimes, these themes help promote the purpose of your story, so the audience can better understand why you told it. Also, be mindful of the necessity to rehearse your stories. Even if the story is fresh in your mind as a lived experience, make sure to practice it several times. Sometimes, when we get in front of people, the setting up of events or the describing of characters makes us nervous or forgetful—which may cause us to ramble. The best solution for this—practice. If your story is too personal/sensitive, be cautious of using it in a speech. Although it may be a perfect example to connect the audience with your topic, sharing something so personal may cause you to become emotional in the moment while sharing. One example, a past speaker gave a presentation about cancer preventatives and shared a story about her mother going through chemotherapy treatments. Unfortunately, while speaking about her mom, the speaker broke down into tears and struggled to finish her presentation.

Storytelling in a Business and Technological World

Many speakers of informative or persuasive speaking style opt to skip their own orally recited story for showing a more modern video. After all, YouTube has been around since 2005, and there is every kind of video imaginable available to viewers. That is just it—YouTube has existed for quite some time, and showing someone else's story in a video is not as novel as it was when first created. Be very careful when attempting to use video to tell a story. It can detract from your own narrative, upstage, or outshine you, and leave the audience wondering the purpose of its placement within your presentation. Make sure the video stories you choose have purpose and do not detract from the message you are trying to convey. Also, make sure you explain the video and the why you chose it for this particular portion of your presentation. Keep the video brief - remember you are the focus of the presentation.

Beyond videos, some may say that stories do not belong in business communication. This is simply not true. If you are in HR, what is the best way to motivate people on policy and procedure? Why, tell them a story of course. Perhaps something happened (good/bad) before and why the presentation today is affected by that situation. If you are in training or sales, stories help move and motivate both your staff and your customers. Marketing, management, finance—you will need to craft a story either visually or verbally. Overall, remember that stories move us and they have a place in business communication in a technological world. Look for examples like those we see in TED talks and you will be on your way to crafting a meaningful story.

Hopefully, you have a better understanding of the goals of an informative speech, the multitude of topic options available, and some important factors to consider as you prepare your speech. Remember the point is to introduce new information to your audience and possibly teach them something at the same time! Consider the time available for your presentation, who will be in the audience (and their experience level), and the expectations for both you and the individuals listening to the information. With these ideas you will create and deliver a great informative message!

REFERENCES

Galbraith, D. D. & Fouch, S. E. (2007). Principles of adult learning: Application to safety training. *Professional Safety, 52*(9), 35–40.

Kennedy, R. C. (2003). Applying principles of adult learning: The key to more effective training programs. *FBI Law Enforcement Bulletin, 72*(4), 1–5.

May, K. T. (2013, December 16). The 20 most popular TED Talks, as of December 2013. [Blog post]. Retrieved from: http://blog.ted.com/the-most-popular-20-ted-talks-2013/.

Palis, A. G. & Quiros, P. A. (2014). Adult learning principles and presentation pearls. *Middle East African Journal of Ophthalmology, 21*(2), 114–122.

Chapter
10 Persuasive Communication

To understand persuasion and persuasive presentations, it is important to have a basic historical understanding of where the field began.

© ibreakstock/Shutterstock.com

Rhetoric is defined "In the classical tradition, the art of persuasion in modern times extended to the art of using language in a way to produce a desired result in an audience" (Woodson, 1979, p. 50). Basically, how do we use our symbols (primarily language) to convince our audience that our point of view is correct? Cooper (1932) included a great quote about figuring out how to persuade an audience. He stated, ". . . the speaker or writer must know the nature of the soul he wishes to persuade. That is, he must know human nature, with its ways of reasoning, its habits, desires, and emotions, and must know the kind of argument that will persuade each kind of men . . ." (p. 13). Once again, audience analysis plays a pivotal role in preparing for a presentation.

The concept of Rhetoric began thousands of years ago in Greece. The fifth century B.C. began a period where rhetoric became more important to the citizens (Kennedy, 1980). The major change was in the use of democracy, particularly in the legal system. There were not any lawyers to present on your behalf, so it became imperative to know how to present and defend your point of view to a jury. Just like today, although books were available to learn different techniques, most people learned better from an actual expert or teacher. One of the first groups were the sophists. "The word **sophist** is derived from the adjective *sophos*, meaning 'wise,' and might be translated 'craftsman'" (Kennedy, 1980, p. 25).

One of the key beliefs taught by the Sophists was that "truth is relative". Have you ever heard the saying, "there's no capital T truth." It is the same concept. The idea is that there is no absolute truth, that everything has a different perspective based on the audience. Think back to our earlier discussion about perception and first impressions.

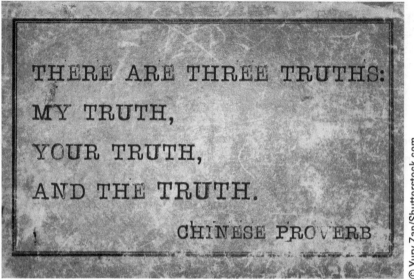

THERE ARE THREE TRUTHS:
MY TRUTH,
YOUR TRUTH,
AND THE TRUTH.

CHINESE PROVERB

© Yury Zap/Shutterstock.com

What one person believes to be "truth" may be completely different from another individual. Have you ever been in or witness to a car accident? Think about what the police do to try and discover what happened. Do they group everyone together to ask questions or interview each person individually? Chances are they collect information from each person one at a time. Think about perspective. One person across the street may notice different details than the person directly behind the accident. It does not mean that one person is "wrong" about what they witnessed, they just have a different "truth". That is why individual interviews are so important because another person stating what they saw may influence what another person witnessed. They may doubt their own account of the accident and not report their details, which could be extremely important when trying to understand what happened. So how does this relate to the Sophists? In essence, the Sophists believed that if you were well trained in how to present an argument, you could convince your audience that your "truth" is the way they should also see the world.

Aristotle's *Rhetoric* is viewed as one of the foundational works in regards to rhetoric and persuasion (Kennedy, 1980).

© Ververidis Vasilis/Shutterstock.com

The third section of the Aristotle's text focused on how to organize a speech, modes of delivery, and how to persuade audiences. The text also broke down specific elements, or "proofs", used to construct arguments. In layman's terms, a **proof** is a form of evidence used in persuasion, and Aristotle broken down proofs into two categories: Inartistic proofs and Artistic proofs. **Inartistic proofs** refer to physical or hard evidence. Think about your courtroom drama on TV today – what types of physical evidence is presented to make a case? Contracts, DNA, fingerprints, etc. would all be examples of inartistic proofs. Basically, the speaker does not necessarily have to argue a perspective because the evidence exists for he/she to find and present.

On the other hand, you have **artistic proofs**, which are created by the speaker. Artistic proofs break down into three types and most people are already familiar with the terms: ethos, logos, and pathos.

Ethos refers to ethics or credibility of the speaker, and the important thing to remember is that ethos is a two-way street. Yes, a speaker may seem trustworthy based on their credentials and education; however, they also have to convince their audience of their credibility during the presentation. Remember we discussed establishing credibility in an earlier chapter. Despite your education and training, if you walk up to a podium and exclaim, "Ugh, I am not prepared for today . . ." do you think the audience will believe you are credible to give a presentation? **Logos**, or logical appeals, is the use of truth and evidence to form conclusions. There is an entire chapter of this text dedicated to finding quality research to use within your presentations. Outside references would be a great tool to use to present a logical argument to your audience. Think about all of the research, facts, and statistics others have already discovered on your topic! It might be a convincing argument for an audience member to realize that it is not just you who believes a certain point of view, but that scientists, researchers, other authors, etc. have come to the same conclusion. Finally is **pathos** or emotional appeals. The presenter tries to make the audience experience feelings regarding the topic, whether it be anger, pain, joy, sadness, etc. A great example would be the animal adoption commercials on tv or adoption drives happening at our local pet shops. Poor, sad, animals locked in cages who just need someone to love them. . . . ugh! How many of us see these animals and want to take them all home?

The key with both inartistic and artistic proofs is to include a good mixture of everything. Each audience member will have different expectations and need a variety of information to be convinced. We began the chapter with a quote by Cooper (1932) stating that persuading an audience requires knowing an audience's "...reasoning, habits, desires, and emotions, and must know the kind of argument that will persuade each kind of men..." (p. 13). Some folks might be numbers-driven and expect lots of facts and figures. Others are bored by numbers and need to see the human element to understand the impact. Diversity in your argument is key, which will also improve your level of ethos with the crowd. Including an assortment of proofs means you considered a variety of different audience members and what information they need to persuade their thinking.

Although thousands of years have passed since the initial works of early scholars, we use these same approaches and foundations when it comes to persuading audiences even today. We know rhetoric refers to the art of persuasion, but the makeup of rhetoric derived from Aristotle, Socrates, Cicero, and so many others to form what is known as the **Five Canons of Rhetoric** (Woodson, 1979).

Invention

Invention is the first of the canons and rightfully so. What is the first thing you have to do if you are going to prepare a persuasive presentation? You might want to know what arguments are already out there about your topic! **Invention**, *inventio*, is all about discovery. This is your initial step into any assignment or task you receive. What have people already said about this issue? Are there any holes in the research? What are the major arguments for and against my point of view?

Arrangement

Arrangement was also known as *dispositio* or form. Put simply, in what way are you presenting and organizing your information? Of course you could prepare a speech, but in what other formats could you try and persuade an audience? Songs, commercials, social media ads, etc. are all options for different arrangements.

Style

Style has a variety of definitions when it comes to the canons of rhetoric that are specific down to the words and as vague as the person actually speaking. The simple way to view **style**, *elocutio*, involves audience analysis. The choices you make is word use, the need to define terminology, etc. and is based upon who you are speaking to. Are the individuals experts on your topic or is this brand new information? The style should adapt so that your audience can, at the very least, understand the message.

Memory

Memory is the canon that has changed the most since the early days of rhetoric. *Memoria* refers to literally the memorization of the information to deliver to an audience. Over time, and with the increased use of technology, the need to memorize a presentation greatly decreased. As discussed in other chapters, memorizing a speech is not necessarily the best approach anymore.

Delivery

Delivery focuses on how the individual presents their message and the skill set required to send the information. **Delivery**, or *pronuntiatio*, could truly examine all of the other canons coming together to produce a well thought-out message to distribute to an audience. Delivery looks at the choices made, the format of the message, and how well they send a message.

Hostile Audience Presentations

Although few people would say that public speaking is an enjoyable experience, the hostile audience is probably one of the toughest speaking situations out there. Larry Tracy (2005) had a great quote in his "Taming Hostile Audience" article that states "...you are not a true professional if you are only capable of speaking to groups that agree with you" (p. 307). This definitely applies to the business environment in various ways. Think about when supervisors have to deliver "bad news". What if your company purchased new software that both you and your team believed did not work the best out of all the options available? As a leader, you still have to professionally move forward with the decisions that may be questionable to you personally.

Who Are You Persuading?

The website changingminds.org discussed four different types of audiences we may face with a persuasive presentation: hostile, critical, uniformed, and sympathetic. Each type of audience has different needs as to what approach and type of information they expect or what will convince them of your point of view.

Hostile

There are multiple reasons why an audience may be "hostile" to your presentation. Boredom, not interested in the topic, angry about news/decisions in the organization, or they just do not like you. These are definitely tough audiences to face! Unfortunately, if you're in a leadership position you will have to bite the bullet and face this crowd. Avoid beginning with the "sales pitch" of how you are going to change everyone's minds about your topic. The hostile audience will immediately respond – "no you're not", and you have lost your crowd before you really even started. It is ok to challenge your audience's beliefs, but be sure to have research ready to refute their arguments. In the end, you may need to leave your audience with no option but to do what you are asking.

"Better let me lead off the presentation."

© Cartoon Resource/Shutterstock.com

Critical

This group believes themselves to be knowledgeable and probably more informed than you on the topic. They will nit-pick and analyze everything you present. The audience will need proof of what you are saying, so stick to research and facts to validate your arguments. Avoid embellishing or making assumptions about the future. Presenting both pros and cons may help persuade this audience.

Uniformed

The uniformed audience may be easier to persuade when compared with the hostile and critical ones. This group does not have all the information so first you will need to discover the knowledge base of the crowd. Do they have basic understanding on your topic or do you need to break down your information to grasp the concepts? The audience wants to understand the full picture so give them the research and details to fill in the blanks. Supervisors may struggle with presenting to the uniformed audience when it is a topic that has been discussed among leadership for an extended time. Although management circles debated the issue for days, weeks, month, etc. realize that the uninformed audience is hearing the information for the first time. It is important to remain patient, answer questions, and explain how the decision was made.

Sympathetic

The easiest of all to persuade! Members of this audience may already be on your side, which helps to convince others of your perspective. A personal approach is great with this group. Show them you are in the same boat, the information impacts you too, and ask for their help moving forward. Pathos appeals work great in this situation.

Dealing with the Unreceptive Audience

Find Common Ground

When we deal with tough audiences, there are some ways we can calm down the situation before we even begin. Before you have to present your message, Tracy (2005) advises to develop some rapport and common ground with your audience. Interact with the crowd and find out what their concerns are. What has them upset or angry? Do you have anything in common with them? Not only does this make you appear concerned with their perspective, it gives you inside information about what you need to cover in your own presentation. If you know the gripes, you want to address them as soon as possible. Holding a meeting where the issues are not addressed will only fuel the fire and raise anxiety.

Have a Clear Objective and Be Prepared

You know what you have to present, but what is your overall goal for the presentation? Are you sharing new information, are you trying to persuade the use of a new product, or delivering bad news? Remember this audience has to be "sold" on whatever you are presenting, so have a clear purpose in mind as you get ready, which is part two. You have a goal, now how are you going to get there? Conduct your research and gather as much information as you can about the situation. What types of questions might the audience ask? What are the major arguments against your point of view? Granted we cannot always prepare for EVERY scenario, but the more possibilities you review, the better presenter you will be in the moment.

Stick to the Facts

For a moment, think about breaking news reports that you have watched on television or appeared online. How much information is shared? How many times do they say, "this is what we know now" or "we don't want to speculate about the situation"? You need to take the same approach as a presenter. Despite all your practice and preparation, you may get questions you do not know the answer to or cannot reveal discussions taking place behind the scenes. Going through "what if" scenarios may cause additional stress on your audience, so stick to your presentation that you prepared. If you do not know the answer to a question, then acknowledge you cannot address it in the moment. Never lie! As time passes you may be able to reveal more information but, in the moment, keep your presentation focused on the data you know and can share. Types of presentations will be discussed further in another chapter.

Stay Calm

For you, as the presenter, you have to maintain your composure (Tracy, 2005). This may be the hardest part of speaking to an unreceptive audience. Maybe you agree with the audience's perspective but, unfortunately, sometimes you are the supervisor and have to pass down the information from a higher power. Other times your audience may interrupt and become verbally aggressive. You cannot fire back! Although the desire to "fight back" burns inside, it will not help the situation. No one wins in those types of interactions. So how do you get out of the situation? The Toastmasters Organization provides some useful tips for dealing with the interruption.

1. Include the audience in your response. If the interactions continue to go back and forth and the interrupter is unsatisfied, you can say something along the lines of "We can discuss this further after the presentation but I'm sure other audience members have questions they would like to ask". Most times, the audience is annoyed by one person monopolizing their time, so will side with you in moving forward.
2. Ask for their name. Unfortunately many people believe they have more power and ability to act aggressively face-to-face and online if they are anonymous. Ask for the person's name so you can respond to them directly by name and remove some of the "freedom" to say whatever they would like.
3. If nothing else works, then end your presentation. Usually the Q&A sessions with the audience occur at the end anyways; so, you can state "unfortunately this is the end of our time but I am available for questions afterwards" and you can remain after the presentation or provide contact information so audience members can follow up if needed.

Persuasive Patterns and Strategies

Monroe's Motivated Sequence

One of the most important things to acknowledge when creating persuasive arguments is they involve strategy. It takes prepared thought, research, and strategy to set up an argument for success. The good news: people have been doing this since childhood. Think about that. You know what way to request a new toy from dad versus mom. Perhaps you told dad he could play with you once the toy was successfully purchased. Perhaps you told mom that the toy was on sale and she would be saving some money. This small example happens throughout childhood and into professional lives. Here, we outline what is called the Motivated Sequence — a strategic step-by-step organizational pattern for creating persuasive change.

Monroe's Motivated Sequence was created by Alan H. Monroe at Purdue University in the 1930s. The purpose is to psychologically move the listener to an outcome of action. The process includes five steps that must always be presented in the same order: attention, need, satisfaction, visualization, and action. Here, we will highlight the purpose of each step within the sequence and ultimately your argument.

Attention

The attention step has a two-part purpose. It first draws attention to the speech event with the traditional attention-getting devices. It then has a secondary purpose to draw attention to the "issue" at hand. Here, you may include facts, stats, anecdotes, stories, etc. The goal often is to show the audience that the issue/topic/thesis is an important and necessary one. Remember to be clear about what the thesis is, your purpose on talking about this subject, and to include a preview of the overall presentation.

Need

The need step creates the need for the listener to be interested and invested in your issue or topic. Why do they NEED to care and why do they NEED to take action. This step includes statistics, stories, metaphors, and many sources to compel the audience to find value in taking action on you issue or thesis. The speaker will create her case here for the listeners to really need to take part in the speech and process.

Satisfaction

The satisfaction step begins to lay out what will happen if the audience chooses to side with your thesis and persuasion. This section highlights the benefits of your speech and topic. It sometimes helps students to think of the need step as a "problem" step and the satisfaction step as a "solutions" step. Another way to think of this step is as a results step. If the audience does XYZ, they can expect ABC (satisfaction) to happen. The satisfaction step demonstrates the efficacy and feasibility of the outcomes of the presentation and its possible effect on the audience.

Visualization

This step paints a mental picture of what will (or will not happen) when the audience participates in the persuasive outcomes. This is story-telling and its power to persuade. Here, the presenter "paints a picture" through story about what the future will or will not look like if the audience follows the recommended persuasive steps. One very careful notation here is that the presenter puts the audience as the center character of the story, not himself of herself. This is important so that the audience feels like they are part of the story.

Action

The action step is the fifth and final step in the process. This step has two main parts just as the attention step. The first is to lay out the step-by-step process of what the audience needs to do to make the persuasion happen. Let us say you are persuading your audience to vote for a candidate. The action step is not simply "now go vote." Instead, you must give your audience baby steps to make the action take place. This may include thought, learning, research, discussion, minor steps, etc. Little bits of action on the way to a larger movement are still pieces of persuasion in the overall larger persuasive request.

The second part of the action step is to, just as the attention step did, conclude the presentation mechanically. To do this, you must remind the audience of the overall points of the presentation, the specific thesis you want them to follow, and to end memorably with a reiteration of the attention-getting devices.

Here is an example that is more specific that may help understand the steps:

Red Wine Company

Attention:

Draws Attention to the ISSUE/TOPIC. Load this section with shocking facts, stats, background material, and evidence. For your speech on wine, you draw attention to the good statistics published about wine, how stressed Americans are, why Americans need to save more money, etc. You have a solution for this stress, this financial damage—it's called red wine.

Need:

What NEEDS does your audience have that your issue pertains to? For example, you have done some research and 45% of your audience is STRESSED out. Perhaps, persuading them to drink your wine will help this NEED.

This section is not necessary directly related to why they NEED to listen to you. It is about the audience's needs, not yours. Think about this. This section is difficult. You have to CREATE the NEED.

Satisfaction:

This is the section that highlights what will happen if they buy into your idea/topic/concept. So, if they are in fact stressed, and they do use your company's wine to relax, they will THEN be more productive at work. Again, work and wine have nothing to do with each other. You are leading the audience to a more relaxing life and a more productive day at work by getting them to buy your wine. Finding statistics about how productive people are when they get rest will bolster this section.

Visualization:

Here is where you TELL A STORY to paint a mental picture of what will or will not happen when they buy into your idea. This is NOT where you show visuals, you story tell.

Action:

The action step is not simply, "now go to redwine.com and order a case of wine." It is MUCH more detailed than this. Help them do research. Tell them where they can get more information. SHOW THEM what it takes to make this happen. This is a detail-oriented section, so, don't rattle off websites and phone numbers . . . provide handouts, request that your audience write things down!

As you begin to formulate the framework for your persuasive outline and presentation, consider the following:

Persuasive Speech Worksheet

TOPIC: _____

THESIS: _____

Claim(s)

Warrant(s)

Evidence

Attention:
Draw attention to the issue. Remember stats, facts, anecdotes, stories.

Need:
Related audience need 1)

Related audience need 2)

Related audience need 3)

Specific Sources

Satisfaction:
What will the audience get out of believing you?

Point 1)
Maybe use evidence, examples, etc.

Point 2)
Use reasoning: logic, fact, emotion

Point 3)
Use statistics, etc.

Visualization:
Start your story here:

Action: What specific steps will the audience take to make your topic happen? Start small and realistic and build up!

Persuasion Skill-Drill Worksheet

Motivated Sequence

Attention: Includes Hook, Thesis (claim) Preview, Credibility	Hook: Thesis: Attention to issue: Preview: Credibility:
Need: (Like Problem) Why does audience NEED to heed your speech/topic/cause/issue?	LOGIC: FACT: VALUE: EMOTION:
Satisfaction: What will Solve/help/alleviate the NEED/issue Go beyond simple scope of problem/solution, really apply to audience's condition. Apply parallel structure!	LOGIC: FACT: VALUE: EMOTION:
Visualization: Paint a good/solid/mental picture of what will/will not happen if the audience buys-in to your speech/call to action	Be vivid, be realistic, use hyperbole too, can even include slides/pictures (but not necessary)
Action: REAL action STEPS (not a final solution like, "now stop smoking." Research, thoughts, steps! Also conclude: Re1 Re2 Re3	Step 1 Step 2 Step 3 Step 4

Alternative Formatting

We have discussed the Motivated Sequence as a way to offer an audience a strategy and moving an audience to action. While all persuasion should have some outcome, the next two patterns work best for issues that are more obvious. Here we will discuss the Problem–Solution format and the Comparative Advantages format.

The Problem–Solution format works when the audience can easily see that the thesis/topic/issue is, in fact, a problem. So, this strategy may not work with all audiences, especially hostile ones mentioned earlier. For example, "nonrecognition of birthdays in the workplace" may not seem like a "problem" to a room full of middle- to upper-level managers who are trying to keep the business going. So, it is absolutely imperative to know your audience when working in the Problem–Solution format. Another example might be content in foods. Someone may give this as a problem/solution presentation, but for the fit people in the audience, their time may feel wasted — so keep all of these variables in mind.

There are two major ways to set up the Problem–Solution format. The first is point-by-point and the second is all points-all solutions.

Point-by-Point

This is where a speaker sets up minipoints that support the greater thesis. For example, the thesis could be "pollution in the nearby river."

Problem 1: the wildlife
Solution 1: X

Problem 2: the smell
Solution 2: Y

Problem 3: the hazards
Solution 3: Z

Of course, each of these topics could possibly be their own speech depending on time and purpose. However, for the larger thesis of pollution — this would be acceptable.

All-Points

This is where the speaker creates a very large problem by creating one major problem from subpoints. It is much like the structure above, except the solutions manifest themselves in a larger second-half of the presentation. For example:

Problem:
  Point 1
  Point 2
  Point 3

So, we have several solutions to rectify these issues.

Solution 1

Solution 2

Solution 3

Remember when working in these structures to employ the same considerations of the true introduction that includes attention-getters, thesis, preview, and credibility statements. As well as a proper subconclusion after your solutions that include the RE3 statements of restating the thesis, points, and attention-getter thus, creating a nice conclusive statement.

The last format we will discuss is the Comparative Advantages strategy. This places options side-by-side and offers a reason for the audience to choose one over the other. The difference between this and the Problem–Solution format is that there may not always be a "problem" in this form of persuasion. For example, you may be pitching one of your products against another and there is nothing wrong with the competition. You simply wish to show how yours is better. This pattern works somewhat like the compare and contrast strategy used in many writing classes. Your strategy should look something like this:

Our product has

X and theirs has Y,

X is better for reasons

1

2

3

Our product has A and theirs has B,

A is better for reasons

1

2

3

So, in short, because of X and A, it would benefit you to choose our product for your next widget.

There are some challenges to using this strategy well and the most important is knowing your audience. One must not say, "ours is cheaper" so, therefore, you should want it — because cost may be of no object to your audience. Things like this will get a speaker into trouble, if she is not careful to know her audience. The other major thing to consider is to compare things worth comparing. For example, if your option has different features and outcomes when compared to other products, why couldn't an audience member choose your product AND something else? Comparative Advantages presentations do not always have to be "all or nothing" type speeches either. In some cases, it could be persuading to choose yoga over running for the benefits you are about to explain. However, there are some people in the audience who are healthy enough and have enough time to do both running AND yoga. So, keep in mind that this strategy does not have to result in a win–lose outcome. The main thing to consider is you will "win" if people chose to support your thesis and go with what you offered. As with all strategies, remember to have a proper introduction and conclusion mentioned above.

Today's Technological World

Making quality strategic arguments over Zoom and through the computer has never been more important. In many cases it takes more time to prepare quality strategic communication intended to be received online, privately, through a technological device.

Careful consideration should be used when thinking about how your audience feels about the topic, what your thesis is, and how you will reveal it through a computer meeting. One-on-one, or group calls still need elements of a traditional phone call where the speaker needs to introduce themselves and welcome everyone. Then, though, the traditional elements of speech are still needed to make sure the persuasive strategy is intentional.

Speakers using persuasion online need to make sure their audience is engaged and paying attention the the message. This calls to questions elements of having cameras on, asking participants questions, checking in through the chat feature, and recapping often. You as the speaker will want to make sure not to read information to an audience when they can read themselves.

Finally, it is important to have a clear call to action in the ending of a Zoom or video presentation. Make sure to recap and revisit your thesis. Make sure people understand what you are asking them to do, and definitely use the platform by offering your contact information and more links to the topic at hand.

This chapter introduced persuasion and its strategies for business communication. The opening discussed a short history to the roots of persuasion and we conclude here with structure to strategy when formulating your persuasive messages. Remember, as the speaker, you need to decide which persuasive presentation pattern is best for you: Monroe's Motivated Sequence, Problem–Solution, or Comparative Advantages. From there, you will form your outline and speakers notes based on your research and the necessary strategy. The number one thing to remember is that persuasion needs research, reference, and a strategy. Many people simply talk about a topic and hope the audience sees the need for it to be important. Often, this falls into an informative presentation that simply lists the points of an item or issue but does not connect the need for the audience to take action. Remember, almost all persuasion should end in some action or thought.

REFERENCES

Cooper, L. (1932). *The Rhetoric of Aristotle*. Englewood Cliffs, NJ: Prentice-Hall, Inc.

DeLazier, S. (n.d.). Defusing a Hostile Audience. Retrieved March 15, 2017 from http://westsidetoastmasters .com/article_reference/defusing_a_hostile_audience_2002-09.html

Four Audiences (n.d.). Retrieved March 23, 2017, from http://changingminds.org/techniques/general /four_audiences.htm

Kennedy, G. A. (1980). *Classical Rhetoric and Its Christian and Secular Tradition from Ancient to Modern Times*. Chapel Hill, NC: The University of North Carolina Press.

Tracy, L. (2005) *Vital Speeches of the Day*. Vol. 71 Issue 10, p306–312.

Woodson, L. (1979). *A Handbook of Modern Rhetorical Terms*. Urbana, IL: National Council of Teachers of English.

http://changingminds.org/techniques/general/four_audiences.htm.

http://westsidetoastmasters.com/article_reference/defusing_a_hostile_audience_2002-09.html.

11 Citing Sources in a Digital World

You are assigned to prepare a presentation and have to include outside references to support your speech. You go to the web, do a quick Google search, and use the first three web links provided – done right? Wrong! Although the Internet makes searching for references easier, it does not guarantee accuracy or quality. This chapter will cover different types of references available and assessing whether the information is appropriate to use in your own work.

Thankfully the days of hunting through the stacks and scanning microfiche are over. Some of you might not know the "joy" of using a card catalog or standing at the copy machine for hours for copies of articles to take home to read. Advances in technology increased the ease of finding and scanning for research from all types of sources including newspapers, journal articles, and web sources.

© antstang/Shutterstock.com

Types of References

Although the Internet can make finding research easier, it does not always mean it is the best option. In addition, some of your professors may require you to use a variety of research beyond the ".com" format. So what are the options available? There are five different categories of references to think about incorporating into your work.

Personal Knowledge and Experience

Do not forget about your own knowledge on your topic! It is a great addition to a presentation to hear something personal from the presenter on the issue. Keep in mind, however, that if your assignment calls for outside research you-yourself will not count as a source. That does not mean leave out your two cents though. Remember we discussed the use of pathos as a great appeal to use in a presentation? Your personal experience can add that emotional touch needed in a speech. It also builds your credibility as a speaker by allowing the audience to understand your connection to a particular presentation topic.

© BearFotos/Shutterstock.com

Library

There is this amazing building on your campus (and probably within your community) where you have access to find information, AND there are people available to help you with your research. Want to know something even more amazing? You may not even have to set foot in this building to access thousands of books, journals, magazines, newspapers, you name it. Definitely check out your local libraries to see how much data are available. Thanks to technology, different types of print media are digitized for easier consumption. Books, journals, etc. can be expensive to print, so often publishers limit printing, but they create digital versions for subscribers to access, including schools. Check with your librarians to see what is accessible to use. Also, ask the librarians for help! No they will not prepare your presentation for you; however, they are experts at finding information, knowing what to search for, and what resources are maintained in the library. Just like with your professors, do not be afraid to ask them questions!

Interviews

Talking with someone about your topic can be a great addition to your presentation. There are two types of testimony you can gather from an interview: expert testimony and lay testimony. Expert testimony is from a person who is experienced, knowledgeable, and/or trained about your subject matter. If you were conducting a speech about cancer treatments, then an interview with an oncologist would be a great example of expert testimony. The second type is lay testimony, which comes from an individual with a unique experience with the subject but not necessarily be an "expert" on the topic. It is based only on personal opinion or experience and not on research or study specifically on the topic. Think about stories you have viewed on the news; let's use an example like when bad weather is approaching. The story includes detailed information about what to expect, timing, etc. from a meteorologist (expert testimony) and interviews with community members on how they are preparing for the storm (lay testimony). There are several steps to keep in mind when deciding to conduct an interview.

1. Determine the Purpose – Do not just interview someone for the sake of an additional source. Be sure that information from this person would really be valuable to your speech. Who is this person? What are their credentials? If the interview does not produce the information you need, then do not settle; move on to another source.
2. Schedule/Plan – Make an appointment with the person you want to speak with versus unexpectedly showing up at their place of work. Remember they have busy schedules too! Before you go, have a set of questions prepared that you want to ask him/her, so you are not trying to think up questions on the spot. It is ok to ask follow-up questions or other ideas in the moment, but you want to have an organized plan of what information you are seeking from this individual. It might be a good idea to provide your questions (or at least what you are hoping to learn) to the individual so they can prepare answers and gather materials beforehand.
3. Conduct Interview – Be on time (if not a little early), ask your questions, stay within your allotted scheduled time, and gather the information you need.
4. Follow-Up – It is always nice to let the interviewee know how your presentation went. Whether an email or a letter (which is a nice personal touch), thank him/her for their time, talk about how you used the information in your speech, and if you know the outcome such as the final grade. Following up also shows respect for the individual and may serve as a great networking tool for you in the future.

Special Interest Groups/Organizations

As you conduct research, you may discover different groups whose sole purpose is research, advocating, or fundraising specifically on your topic. Think about if you were conducting research about breast cancer; there are numerous nonprofit organizations dedicated to the cause such as the American Cancer Society, Susan G. Komen, and so many others. Not only do organizations maintain websites with useful information, but also may have local branches within communities for you to schedule an interview and visit with an actual representative. Normally, organizations are grateful that outsiders express interest in learning more about their group and happy to share materials to promote their work.

© David Carillet/Shutterstock.com

Internet

Although this may be the first place you go to conduct research, it does not guarantee accuracy. Websites can provide quick and useful information to incorporate into your research, but there are several aspects to consider before citing an Internet source.

Evaluating Web Sources

Even though conducting research is easier, the need to evaluate references increased. There is one easy question to ask when determining the value of a source. . . . is it CRAAP? California State University published a great breakdown of what to assess when looking for quality outside research.

Currency

Look at when the information was published or posted online. Was the article released recently? When was the last time the website was updated? Depending on your project, current information may be necessary. A good rule of thumb is to search within the last 10 years; however, if you need a historical background you would obviously go farther back in your search. Think about doing a presentation on technology – how much has changed in 10 years? Depending on the topic, you may want to search and find the most recent information available.

Relevance

Is this the best research for your project or was it the first thing you found? Remember organizations pay to have their websites pop up first on search engines. What audience is the author targeting? This happens a lot when conducting research. We find a title that sounds perfect for what we need, but as we start reading the article it has nothing to do with our topic at all. You want to be sure the material is the best fit for your presentation.

Authority

Who wrote the article? On what type of website did you find it? The authority examines whether the person or organization has the qualifications to write on the subject matter. You will usually find qualifications, additional research, etc. to justify their position. This is why you really need to question using a blog as a source. Is it really someone credible or just a random person posting their two cents about the topic? Also check out the website address -.com,. edu,. gov,. net,. org. That will also tell you something about the authority of the information.

Accuracy

How reliable is the information? Is other research cited or is it a first-person perspective? Look at the quality of the information. It would be a red flag to find spelling and grammar mistakes throughout the article. Also, look to see if the research has been peer-reviewed. Some work you complete may require the use of peer-reviewed or scholarly research. Often this refers to academic journals where scholars in the same field review an author's work to verify the research is top notch before it is accepted for publication.

Purpose

Why was the information produced? Is there a bias or is it objective? Are they trying to sell something? Major companies and organizations often have goals to achieve. You want to be sure that the research you use is not slanted to just their position. Reviewing other publications from the same source could reveal if there is an agenda.

If any of these items are in question when reviewing your research, then it might be best to move on to another source. Remember, you are putting together your own presentation, so you do not want to be called into question about the references you use. Having quality research also raises your credibility and authority to present on the topic.

Now to discuss the "evil" Wikipedia. Granted you probably do not want to cite "according to Wikipedia . . ." in any of your work unless your goal is to get a laugh from your audience. The reason Wikipedia, and many other online sources, get a bad rap is because the information can be altered. Yes, the website is maintained and updated regularly, but the chance the information is incorrect exists. However, Wikipedia serves as a great starting place when conducting research. After finding information through Wikipedia, if you will scroll to the very bottom of the page, you will often find a References section for the information. Those are the sources you need to go find for yourself!

Many times, you will find authors cite references within their articles just like your requirements. If you find that the information they cited would be useful in your own presentation, then research to find that original article instead of trusting the Wikipedia author cited the information correctly. This is referred to as a secondary source (APA). The Publication Manual of the American Psychological Association (2010) states to "Use secondary sources sparingly, for instance, when the original work is out of print, unavailable through usual sources, or not available in English" (p. 178). This is also referred to as "back-citing" when you do not attempt to track down the original source. You want to ensure that you are quoting material correctly in your own work.

Selecting the Best Supporting Material

As you conduct research you may find hundreds, if not thousands, of articles about your topic. Feeling overwhelmed is not uncommon, but there are ways to narrow down your search and select the best research for your presentation. Here are some items to keep in mind that may help you make decisions about what data to incorporate.

Think about the *magnitude* of the research you discover. The idea is "bigger is better" is a good rule to remember when evaluating data. Say you find two articles about your topic; one article states that 72% of people are impacted while the other says 85% of individuals feel the effects. You might consider using the research showing more people are affected by the issue. This does not mean you alter the research yourself! Provide the data as presented from the research.

Can you find any data that show results within your surrounding community or state? The *proximity* of research is a great way to show your audience members that your issue hits close to home. It is easy to dismiss research and findings when you do not believe it applies to us. "Who cares what is happening in another state? I live here." Some audience members will want to understand how the information directly impacts their lives; otherwise they may not care.

In the chapter about persuasive presentations, we discussed different appeals we can use to engage our audience. This is also true when it comes to research. You want to use a *variety* of sources and information throughout your presentation. Remember some audience members may prefer the hard-core facts and statistics about a subject. Others want personal examples and stories to show the human impact on the issue. Incorporating a little of everything helps meet all of your audience's needs. In addition, variety also refers to the types of outside research you include. For example, avoid only using Internet sources, only Interviews, etc. You want to show your audience you researched through different avenues and selected the best data for your speech. Using all websites might indicate you did a quick Internet search and simply used the first few links that appeared.

Also be sure to review how *suitable*, or appropriate, your references are for the situation. Remember to consider your audience once again as you make decisions about research. Does your information come from a political source, do they have their own agenda with the data published, is there any concern of bias or "fake news" with your information, etc.? If you are worried about how the audience will receive information from a particular person or organization, then it might be best to select another reference to avoid potential backlash. It is always better to be safe than sorry.

Finally, check your references thoroughly to see how the author(s) report facts and statistics in research. Review the choices made with the *presentation* of information because it is extremely easy to manipulate data and how a reader consumes the evidence. Examine the following charts to see how data are presented.

An initial look at the graphs indicates a huge difference when comparing Figures 1 and 2. Take a closer look at the numbers on the left hand side (the Y-axis). Figure 1 includes a range of 0–6 where Figure 2 only displays 4–6. The same concept is applied to Figure 3. If a person interested in purchasing a home only glanced at the chart, they may decide it was not the correct time to invest because of the "massive increase in house prices". However, Figure 4 shows a breakdown by 10,000 dollars versus every 1,000 dollars. The increase appears less extreme with Figure 4. The point is to be smart consumers of facts, statistics, and visual displays of information.

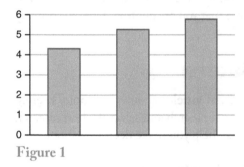

Figure 1

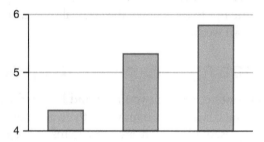

Figure 2

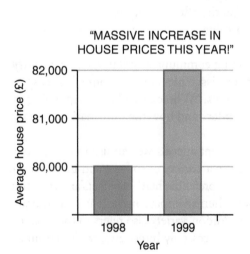

Figure 3

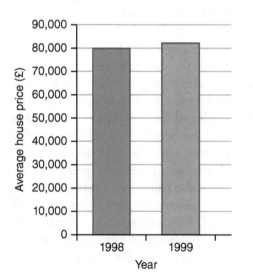

Figure 4

Using References Effectively

So, you found your research, but how do you incorporate it into your paper or presentation? A lot of students question how often they need to reference outside information when integrating it into their own work. Too much is citing with every single sentence, but not enough is not citing anything or waiting until the reference section at the end of a document (if there is one). Balance is the key. When presenting your own thoughts or common knowledge, you do not need to include a reference. However, whenever you do use ideas, quotes, or information that came from another source, you need to give credit to where that information came from. Let your audience know immediately that you are using an outside reference. There are multiple ways to give credit when writing (check your formatting guide, whether it be APA, MLA, etc.) either at the beginning or end of sentences. For instance, "According to this author. . .." "This organization posted research. . .." and be specific when citing. Google is not a source – it is a search engine, and there is a lot of information out there on the web. Make sure your audience is clear about where you discovered the research.

The same is true when giving a verbal presentation; you want to give credit verbally at the moment you present information from your references. Many times, speakers make the mistake of ending their speech with "and these are my references" or listing them on a PowerPoint slide (which we will discuss more in-depth with the visual aids chapter). Just listing your references all at once does not tell the audience what information came from which reference.

FIND CREDIBLE SOURCES
AND CITE THEM.

© bfk/Shutterstock.com

Beautifully Citing Verbal Sources

One of the more frequent questions we receive from speakers newer to the public speaking arena is, "What do I actually say when it is time to use my source in my presentation?" This is absolutely an important and real question because often to this point in school, students have only been required to cite sources in paper documents they hand in/supply to a professor or audience. Of course, this is where the misguided practice of showing a reference slide started. However, we have solutions that will move you to beautiful citation.

First, it is imperative you work the source into a sentence of the presentation that matches the tone, cadence, candor, and quality of the rest of the speeches sentences.

> Like this: In 2009, Steve Smith an economist from Campus University noted the recession of 2008 was the worst since the Great Depression.
> Not this: The 2008 recession was the worst since the Great Depression. Oh, and my source for this is Steve Smith of Campus University in 2009.

The second example is clunky and may take away from the flow of the sentences that will follow. Of course, it too may be "cleaned up" in various ways. This would work:

> The 2008 recession was the worst since the Great Depression. Steve Smith, an economist, from Campus University found this in his 2009 research following the recent stock market crash. He also noted other comparisons such as XYZ.

The secret here is to work references and citations into rehearsed presentation rhetoric so listeners can easily digest and understand the reference point, but not detract from the artistic, professional, and performative beauty of your speech.

The second consideration of citing beautiful sources in a presentation is to choose the two or three most important "touch points" of the reference to verbally cite for your audience. When we say touch points, we are referring to identifying aspects of the reference you are using. In this technological world it is not necessarily important to *orally* provide a complete APA reference to your listeners. This will get cumbersome and clunky. Instead, consider the two to three most relevant parts of the source that would allow your audience to accept its credibility, and possibly research on their own either during or following your speech.

For example: Steve Smith, an economist at Campus University, authored an article titled, "What the 2008 Recession Really Means," in an academic journal named, "The Florida Economist," in 2009, and published in Miami, FL.

> This APA citation would have six pieces of reference, more if you used certain pages numbers or possibly retrieved it via the Web. You as the author/speaker have to choose which elements of the article should be cited verbally in your presentation; keeping in mind the purpose of choosing those touch points. In this case the author, his title, and the year or journal would be 1) enough to find on online and, 2) enough to give credibility to your reference and its support of your overall presentation.

A third necessity to citing sources beautifully within a presentation is to rehearse using those sources in your practice sessions. They should not be afterthoughts or ignored when rehearsing. This can lead you down the "clunky" route when citing sources. Additionally, it is imperative you practice saying authors and proper names that are different from your native language. You do not get a pass by saying, "Michael um, I don't know how to pronounce this, Wascawitzy? or something like that" when citing your sources. No! This is the difference between novice speakers and excellent speakers.

Instead, you should rehearse all names, foreign and domestic, new or old to you, well ahead of time. If the names are complicated to you, it is okay to have them written on your notes and spelled phonetically to your liking. Do not show your audience you are struggling with names. Say them with confidence and the same energy as the easy ones. Research or ask if you do not know how to pronounce an item. If that does not satisfy your pronunciation questions, you should make your best attempt and perfect it. Saying "your version" of a pronunciation with confidence and energy will show your audience you know what you are talking about. As presenters, your author team has never had one person vocally embarrass us during a presentation by calling us out for pronouncing something incorrectly. Many speakers have a fear in their heads of being humiliated in this way, but in reality it happens very little, if at all.

Fourth, accuracy in verbal citation is of utmost importance when citing sources orally. A good practice is to use two–three touch points. At conferences, meetings, and in college classrooms, you have audience members who are jotting down names or researching those sources for use later. You have to get it right!

Recently, in class, there was a student speaker who said in his speech the students of his college campus were among the most attractive of ranked college campuses in the United States. He, however, got the blog source/article incorrect and one audience member stated in the next class that she spent an hour trying to find the list to share with her friends – but to no avail. The student speaker had incorrectly cited his source which affected his claim, and ultimately he got "called out" in class. He was embarrassed and dug through his notes to discover he had mixed a few things up – so badly that his classmate was not able to find the list.

The above example, however simple, highlights the imperative need to get all sourced information correct. Getting in the habit of citing perfect and credible sources will only stand to build your ethos and source credibility of the position you hold – student, employee, leader, manager, owner, as well as the credibility of your organization.

Finally, and most important, be sure you answer the 'why' you included the reference in your presentation. A good way to setup your reference information is the PIE structure:

- **P**oint
- **I**llustration
- **E**xplanation

The Point is where you introduce the outside research to the audience. You state the fact or information you want to audience to know and give credit to your source. With Illustration, you want to provide your audience an example in your own words. Sometimes research articles do not make sense the first time you read them. You may have to conduct further research to understand what the author is saying.

© YURALAITS ALBERT/Shutterstock.com

The audience does not have the opportunity to review the article; they only have the words you present. Therefore, when you present outside research you present the Point, then use Illustration to break it down so what you presented is understood by your audience members. Explanation is your opportunity to showcase why the reference information is important. Make the connection clear between the reference and how it relates back to your topic.

Beautiful source citation is something that master presenters have perfected. Working sources into speech is something very new to many speakers who have relied on a references slide and clunky APA sources on PowerPoint slides mostly unreadable to audience members. This somewhat accepted incorrect practice has misguided speakers for years. By citing proper, credible, and understandable oral citations, a speaker boosts credibility of all things related to her presentation.

The goal of the chapter was to provide you with an understanding of what qualifies as outside research, how to effectively evaluate references, and the best way to incorporate data into your own work. As you continue through college or are already in the workforce, you will soon discover that your own opinions are valuable but not enough. However, if you can add in credible research to back up your points of view, you can more likely convince your audience of the value of your information and your own credibility. Although technology makes conducting research easier, it is not always the best option to incorporate. Do your digging and find the best data to meet your needs—professionally and ethically.

REFERENCE

Evaluating Information – Applying the CRAAP Test (2010). Retrieved March 17 2017, from https://www.csuchico.edu/lins/handouts/eval_websites.pdf

Chapter

12 Visuals in a Virtual World

You completed your research, have all of the information organized and ready to go, but feel like something is missing. Maybe there is a better way to explain difficult concepts to your audience. Perhaps you need to give them something to walk away with to refer back to your presentation later. How are you going to keep your audience engaged during your speech?

© ESB Professional/Shutterstock.com

    A presentation aid may be the solution. There are millions of options when it comes to what aid to choose, how to incorporate them, and using them effectively during a presentation. This chapter will cover the different types of presentation aids available, what to consider when selecting an aid, and focusing how technological options are available for both face-to-face and virtual presentations.

    Let us start off with a basic understanding of **presentation aids**. This could be anything tangible that helps communicate an idea to an audience. Often they are referred to as "visual" aids because people often learn more through sight than any of their other senses. However, a visual aid may not always be the best choice. For example, if you were giving a speech about different genres of music, you might actually play some examples for your audience to hear versus showing pictures of sheet music. There are multiple reasons why a presenter incorporates a presentation aid into their work.

Enhance Understanding

Helping your audience grasp the content you are presenting is probably the number one reason to add in a presentation aid. Sometimes as speakers our words are not enough; however, if I can show you a picture, provide a handout, etc. that could assist in understanding, then my audience is more likely to stay engaged with the content.

Enhance Memory

Not only will your audience understand your information, but they are more likely to remember your presentation long after they have moved on to something else. Think about the number of classes you sit through at school or meetings you have to endure in the workplace. A few days could go by before we start a project discussed in the meeting – how can you assist your audience in remembering the task at hand? A good presentation aid may trigger memory and help complete work more efficiently.

© Trueffelpix/Shutterstock.com

Organize Ideas

Presentation aids help with organization, both for the speaker and the audience. As the presenter, you complete your research and prepare to speak in front of a crowd. However, standing up in front of that group can be nerve-wracking! A good presentation aid serves to keep the speaker on track and pace their presentation. In addition, the audience receives a clear path of what information will be covered and the goals of the speaker. Just make sure when using PowerPoint and other visuals to keep your audience as the target of the presentation aid. Avoid creating a visual script for yourself which is terribly boring for an audience.

© SofiaV/Shutterstock.com

Gain/Maintain Attention

If you have no clue how to begin your presentation or unsure about what to use as an attention-getter, maybe a presentation aid is your best option. You can accomplish two speech goals at one time by grabbing your audience's attention *and* incorporating an effective aid in the same step. Presentation aids are also great to break up a presentation. An audience's attention span is pretty short, so if you have been speaking for a while, it is a good idea to switch gears and incorporate an aid midspeech for your audience to refocus.

Illustrate a Sequence of Events

A presentation aid is an excellent idea if you have to present a new process or step-by-step instructions to a group. It is one thing to "tell" your audience how to complete a task, it is more effective if you can "show" them how to do each step in the process. Lay out the instructions, include screenshots or videos of what comes next, etc. so your audience can easily follow along with the information.

Types of Presentation Aids

So, we discussed the benefits of using aids in our presentations, but what are all the options out there to use? Let us just say it is not a short list! The different types of aids break down into three different categories: two-dimensional (2-D), three-dimensional (3-D), and audio-visual.

2-D Presentation Aids

Some examples of two-dimensional aids include handouts, drawings, photos, maps, etc. Basically, it includes anything on paper for your audience to have in hand. There are some pros and cons to using 2-D aids. Some positives include 1) audience members having something in hand they can take with them after the presentation, 2) everyone can easily see the aid, and 3) they have the ability to make notes directly on the aid. However, there are downfalls to 2-D aids to consider. 1) If you do not know how many people will be in your audience you may not have enough copies for everyone,

© Golden Pixels LLC/Shutterstock.com

2) it is not very economically friendly to print out hundreds of copies of paper, ink, etc., and 3) handouts can be a distraction where the audience is focusing on the information in their hands and not what you are presenting in front of the room.

3-D Presentation Aids

Three-dimensional aids include actual objects, models, and even other people can serve as presentation aids. Think back to your science labs where they had the models of the internal organs you could take out and see where each part of the body was located. Those would serve as 3-D aids. Of course, just like with 2-D, there are positives and negatives to consider. A 3-D image 1) allows the audience to "see" the actual item versus a picture, 2) it allows the audience a hands-on approach to your presentation, and 3) in the case of people, can provide an additional perspective beyond the speaker's own words. However, 1) models can be

© CandyBox Images/Shutterstock.com

difficult for a large crowd to see, 2) the presenter really needs to spend time practicing with the model so he/she knows how it goes together quickly or prepping the guest speakers on what to say, 3) objects in the hands of the audience are an even greater distraction to overcome as they have something to play with during the speech.

Audio–Visual

The last category is probably the most commonly used when it comes to presentation aids. The audio–visual category includes technology use such as sound, movie clips, PowerPoint presentations, etc. There are multiple factors to examine when deciding to incorporate technology into a presentation. On the plus side 1) technology allows for a large-scale audience to consume the media easily, 2) the presenter only has to prepare one aid versus multiple copies, and 3) most presentation spaces are already equipped to allow for multimedia presentations. However, 1) many speakers over-rely on technology to be the entire presentation instead of a tool, 2) there is no guarantee that media will work when uploaded/opened in the presentation space, and 3) the use of audio–visual aids requires more practice than any of the other alternatives. Unfortunately, many speakers underestimate the difficulty of using technology in a presentation, which we will cover more in-depth later in this chapter.

© Matej Kastelic/Shutterstock.com

No matter which type of presentation aid you select, remember to keep it professional. You are either in a college setting or preparing for a work presentation. In addition to being professional, it is imperative to keep your presentation in line with the technological standards of the 2020s and beyond. Even today, so many speakers fall into traps of saying, "I wasn't able to get a picture of . . . XYZ; or, this is a stock photo of a lake, not the actual lake I'm discussing today." These excuses demonstrate nothing more than lack of preparation. If you're going to use a presentation aid to "show" your audience something—then really show them. It takes minimal time to head to Instagram and grab an actual photo of the thing you're discussing, or to head outside and use your iPhone to make a quick video of the place you are covering in your speech. Moreover, if greater understanding is what you're after—you may have to create a graph, graphic, or table.

The days of the poster board and markers are over! It is amazing how many presenters will show up with a rolled poster and then expect it to magically lay flat during their speech. Think professional! Along the professional lines, there are other types of aids that should NEVER cross your mind as a viable option. You would think these would be common sense, but we have all heard the saying, "Common sense is not so common." Do not bring animals, weapons, and/or drug paraphilia as a presentation aid. We know there are some instances that call for those specific types of aids to be used. If you are training in the police academy, you will have access to weapons. However, in your typical classroom and/or business setting, these items are not appropriate. If you have the need to show certain items, use images and not the real thing!

© wavebreakmedia/Shutterstock.com

Guidelines for Using Presentation Aids

No matter which type of aid you decide to use, there are common guidelines (and mistakes) to consider as you prepare your speech.

1. Make it Easy to See – One of the biggest complaints from audience members is the inability to view information presented. Think about the location of each of the individuals in your audience. Will the person in the back row be able to see your aid easily? Remember, if they are straining to see a picture, they are not listening to what you have to say. The solution is not to pass a picture around the room. Your presentation may be finished by the time it reaches the last person.
2. K.I.S.S. – Keep It Simple and Succinct (sometimes it is Keep It Simple Stupid!). Do not spend a lot of time, money, or energy on your presentation aid. Remember it is an element to reinforce your speech – not be the speech entirely!
3. Select the Right Aid – Make the best choice based on your speech topic and your own personal delivery style. Although a 3-D model may seem like the best option, if you are not comfortable putting a model together for the audience to see then maybe it is best to consider alternative aids.
4. Practice with your Aid – There is that crazy word "practice" again. Just as you rehearse your presentation, you must also practice your delivery incorporating your aids. Consider when you are going to use them, how you will present them to the audience, and what you hope to accomplish by including them in the speech.
5. Make Eye Contact with Audience – Remember that you should be the focus for the audience and not your aid. No matter which type of aid you select, you need to practice good delivery skills and keep your eye contact with the crowd. Fumbling with models, reading from screens, etc. reduces your credibility as a speaker who knows their content.
6. Explain Your Aid – If you have taken the time to really think about the proper aid to use in your speech, then you need to emphasize its importance to the audience. There is a reason you selected an image, model, song, etc. to include; be sure to explain that purpose to the audience! In addition, the explanation should not be an afterthought or a closing statement. You, the speaker, need to bring the presentation to a solid conclusion.

"At least he made eye contact this time."

© Cartoon Resource/Shutterstock.com

please follow the instructions

© riedjal/Shutterstock.com

If Anything simply can not go wrong It Will anyway

© astephan/Shutterstock.com

7. Use Handouts Effectively – A lot of beginner presenters are unsure about when to provide their audience members with handouts. They fumble with them at the beginning, kill lots of time trying to pass them out during their presentation, or quickly throw them at their audience as they wrap up their presentations without explanation. The first question to ask yourself is – when does my audience need the handout? That determines when to pass them out. If the information is for the audience to follow along, then pass them out before you begin. If it is something to only refer to midspeech, still pass them out before you begin, but ask the audience to keep them face down until you are ready to refer to the information. If the handout is parting information, then let your audience know what is included on the handout that you will provide after the speech is complete.

8. Control Your Aid – There are many ways to "control" your aid and the audience's use of your instrument. Do not be afraid to instruct your audience on how to act/interact. Tell them to keep the handouts face down until you tell them to review the information. Ask them to move tables/chairs into small groups to work on a model. Let them know you will answer questions about a process after your presentation is complete. We will also address the importance of control in other situations later in this section.

9. Remember Murphy's Law – This is probably the best piece of advice for any presenter to keep in mind as you prepare a speech. Murphy's Law states,

"Anything that can go wrong, will go wrong". What does this mean for you? Always have a backup plan ready to go. What happens if you planned to show a PowerPoint presentation, but the projector is broken in the room? Say you plan to pass out handouts, but you drop them in the mud just minutes before your speech? "Something" always happens on presentation days. However, if you have a backup plan, the chances of something going wrong seem to magically decrease. It is when you do not have a Plan B that disaster strikes.

Shock Value

There is one area to think long and hard about before deciding to use as a presentation aid and that is whether to include shocking and/or graphic materials. We have all heard "sex sells," and we even discussed attention-getters within our text. If you think using such materials is truly the best option for your presentation, then there are a few questions/factors to keep in mind.

1. Is it truly necessary and/or fitting for the speech topic? Just because you may have the ability to shock your audience does not mean you should do so every chance you get. You might have to obtain permission from the individual/group who asked you to speak to ensure they approve.
2. Can YOU handle presenting sensitive material? Sometimes, we are nervous or uncomfortable when graphic images are displayed in our presentation. For example, it is not appropriate to giggle and snicker as a presenter when showing sensitive materials. It kills your credibility if you cannot keep a straight face.

© Annette Shaff/Shutterstock.com

© Aquir/Shutterstock.com

3. Warn Your Audience First. Always allow the audience the opportunity to look away if they do not want to see the images. Although the point is to trigger a reaction, sometimes an audience may be personally connected to the topic and react stronger than expected. Think about showing pictures of aborted fetuses to an audience member who suffered a miscarriage – how might she feel viewing that image? Specifically, tell your audience something along the lines of, "I am about to show some pretty graphic images, so if you do not want to see them, please look away now."

4. Move Past the Shock Factor Quickly. You have warned your audience, you presented the shocking materials, now it is time to get back to your presentation. This means that you need to get the shocking information off of the screen, out of their eyesight, etc. You do not want to leave that content visible through your entire presentation, because you (the speaker) would not be the focus. The audience will stay in a state of shock, grossed out, etc. and not return to your engaged listeners.

5. Triggers. Something we know more about (now more than ever) is the unknown triggering impact of visuals and speeches. Often popular classroom speech topics may be negative for the listeners in the room. Examples of this may be sexual assault, trauma, or campus crime. Sometimes well-meaning students make a presentation on topics not ever considering a victim may also be a classmate or faculty member. While we do not have to be overly politically correct or bland, it is always important to consider the health and safety of your audience members; can you achieve the same awareness or accomplish your goal without causing triggers?

Using Technology As a Presentation Aid

This section is of great importance (and stress) to us authors. We have researched, written, presented, taught workshops, etc. on this issue and yet incorrect use of technology continues to spread like a virus. It is even more frustrating when others within our discipline practice bad habits as it serves as a model for their own students. No matter which program you use (PowerPoint, KeyNote, Prezi, etc.), guidelines about proper implementation are the same. Remember your aid is a tool and not your entire presentation. You should remain the focus when speaking. We briefly discussed pros and cons of audio–visual aids earlier in the chapter, but this section will cover specifically presentation software, creating effective slides, and tips to effective use.

Positives to Presentation Software

Although most people experience the negative aspects of "death by PowerPoint," there are some benefits to implementation.

1. No writing on the board/turning your back to the audience. This is a huge victory for those of us presenters who are left-handed, have terrible handwriting, and/or cannot write in a straight line if our life depended on it! Careful preparation means you can clearly display your text for the audience

members to view quickly and then move on to your next point. They are not waiting on you to write information down or trying to decipher your "hieroglyphics" on the board.

2. Clearly displayed information. It is very easy to manipulate text and imagery on a presentation to enlarge it, so all of your audience members can view simultaneously. No more killing trees with hundreds of copies!

3. Organize Information. Creating presentation slides allows for a clear, linear progression of information. You decide when information appears, in what order, etc. to fit right in with your speech.

4. Appeals to Various Learning Styles. Remember your audience is a really diverse group of individuals. Some prefer to hear information, others want hands on, others still want to actually see information. Slides allow for more variety in your speech. You are talking, the slides show the information, and you could provide a handout for the hands. You have hit all three learning styles efficiently.

5. Retention of Information. By appealing to various senses and learning styles, the audience is more likely to remember your information because you created a well-crafted presentation to gain and maintain their attention.

Negatives of Presentation Software

Despite the positive aspects of technology, unfortunately it is easy to misuse. Here are some of the major pitfalls to remember as you work on your own speech.

1. Bad Speaking Habits–The number one issue people experience with using technology. How many of us sat through a presenter who just read word for word from a slide? Ugh – so frustrating. The typical response is, "I can read, why do I have to sit through this presentation and be read to?" Honestly, it is terrible to sit through that type of situation, so why would you present the same way you despise? Remember the aid is a tool and not the whole story. You should practice good speaking habits no matter what type of aid you employ.

2. Oversimplifies Data. Unfortunately, we have to train our audience to be receptors of good presentations too. There are instances where an audience member thinks, "If it was important, it would

© Romariolen/Shutterstock.com

be included on the slide." However, when the speaker's goal is to be the focal point, the aid serves only as a supplement. A good presentation aid may only include images and mean nothing without having the speaker's content included.

3. Audience Expectations. Although using presentation software is more commonplace, it may not be our first choice to implement into our presentation. Perhaps you think a 3-D example is a better fit for your presentation at a conference. Then you get an email from the conference planner that they want a copy of your PowerPoint in advance. Does this mean so much for your 3-D aid? Not necessarily. However, it may mean that you need to create a presentation to go along with the 3-D aid you planned initially.

Basic Slide Construction

Now that we covered pros and cons, let's discuss the multitude of options you have when it comes to creating your presentation aid. All of the choices can be overwhelming (and time consuming), but it is important to remember the basic premise we keep stressing – keep it simple! Remember YOU are the focus and your aid serves only as a supplement.

Background

How many of us have sat through a presentation that had no color or variety for the entire presentation? Even though the standard is a white slide with black text, there is no creativity involved in this design. In addition, if you have a lengthy presentation, white/bright colors are extremely harsh on your eyes and difficult to focus on for long periods of time. Instead consider a color that is not so bright, but keeps the information clear for the audience to view as well.

Text Selection

Same thing goes with selecting your text. The template may default to Times New Roman, but there are hundreds of different font options available. Whatever font you choose, it needs to be easy for the audience to consume quickly. Nothing too swirly, "cute," crammed together, etc. Remember the audience has to view your information quickly and then return to you as a presenter. Make sure you select

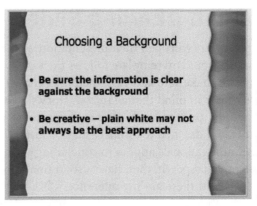

Drawing by Brandy Fair

a font that is an appropriate size for the audience to see as well. One final item to consider is the color of the text. In our blue sample slide above, using a light blue font would be difficult to read. Avoid bright, neon colors for both the background and the text, so you are audience is not blinded. In addition, realize that members of your audience might be color blind, so avoid combinations that leave the audience in the dark.

Limit Text/Graphics

The temptation to read from your slides is greater if you cram them full of information. In addition, you do not want to enrage your audience by reading to them and not presenting additional information beyond the slide. There is no point of sitting through your speech when they could have read the information for themselves on their own. Instead, keep your slides brief and highlight key facts, but leave the rest of your content in your own verbal delivery. Same rule applies to incorporating images into your presentation. Make sure there is a point to using them. Clipart and images are fun to engage your audience, but have a purpose to incorporating images too.

Transitioning between Slides

Different presentation software includes options for how you want your information and images to appear before your audience. Do you want all your text to appear at the same time? Show up line-by-line as you present? You have multiple options. No matter which approach you prefer, there are some options for transitioning to avoid. There is a setting to have text appear letter-by-letter. It takes FOREVER for information to show up so the speaker often sits and waits for everything to appear. Do not leave your audience hanging for information. In addition, avoid transition sounds. It will catch your audience off-guard, but overuse appears childish and annoying. Finally, know when the transitions will occur in your presentation. Speakers often make the mistake of advancing to the next slide and were not ready, or forgetting they have one more item to discuss and not realizing it until they click and are surprised by the information.

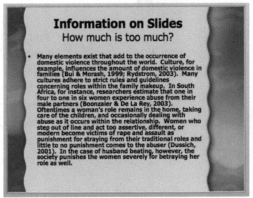

Drawing by Brandy Fair

Beginning/Ending Slides

Many presenters will open their presentation with their title/topic and their name on the opening slide. In addition, the standard template follows the same format. An intro slide is a good idea in conference-type situations to make sure audience members know they are in the correct room to view your presentation. However, keep in mind that an introductory slide takes away from your attention-getter. The first step in your presentation is to "grab" your audience to want to listen. If they already know what is coming based on your title slide, then the impact may be lost.

The same rationale applies to concluding your presentation. You wrap up your points, drive home the purpose of your speech, then have a solid final thought – excellent! Until you make the worst statement ever. . . . . "And these are my references". NEVER have an unxplained, English-paper-style references/works cited slide included in your presentation. Remember we discussed in a previous chapter about citing outside sources as you are presenting them during the speech. Same rule applies for your aid. You can incorporate your references into the slide so you remember to say them. It allows you to give credit (in the moment) to where you found the research, and avoid the list at the end of your speech of your works cited. You lose all of your momentum in closing your speech with that list of sources versus your powerful final thought.

Like we discussed, using presentation software has become a standard when incorporating aids into a speech. Although there are some pitfalls to avoid, it can be a great tool to use. Here are a few additional tips to make the most of your aid.

The 6 x 6 Rule – Keep this rule in mind if you are worried you have too much information included on a slide. No more than 6 lines of text, no more than 6 words per line. We are not saying that you have to count every word on every slide to make sure you have the "proper" amount, but if you can quickly review content without having to stop and read too much, you know you are on the right track.

K.I.S.S. Method – We talked about Keep It Simple and Succinct earlier in this chapter for general presentation aid use. The same method applies specifically to technological software too. Yes, there are lots of bells and whistles that come with using technology, but you are not required to use all of them in a single presentation.

© KJNNT/Shutterstock.com

Handouts Available – Most software includes an option to print your presentation into handout form. This is a good backup in case Murphy's Law strikes and you are unable to show your actual presentation. It allows you to practice with content slides and help the audience follow along and take notes, if necessary.

Hopefully this chapter provided you with useful guidelines and factors to consider when incorporating presentation aids into your speech. We examined different types of presentation aids available, what to consider when selecting an aid, and focusing on what technological options are available for both face-to-face and virtual presentations. Trial and error, along with practice, will make or break using aids to enhance your speech. Just know that a good aid (while practicing goodspeaking habits) really helps take your presentation to the next level.

Chapter

13 Cover Letters, Resumes, and Interviewing

So are you looking for a new position? Feeling overwhelmed about where to start? There are definitely a lot of steps to take when looking for a job, but it can be managed by breaking it down piece-by-piece. No matter what, there will be certain aspects that are the same despite the position, and hopefully this chapter will help you prepare for each step.

Resumes

You have about 10 seconds . . . just 10 little seconds for someone to judge who you are. That is about the average time a potential employer looks at a resume (Frankel, 2016). Since you have such a short amount of time, it becomes extremely important to make the most out of your resume document and your overall image. A **Resume** is a clean, concise, captivating one-page document that highlights specific jobs, education, and skills applicable to a position.

"I would prefer to just look at your resume."

© Cartoon Resource/Shutterstock.com

Hopefully, you have kept up with all of your jobs, accomplishments, awards, etc. throughout your life. If not – it is time to start that master document!!! Often when we apply for jobs, we are looking at a variety of positions that may require different skill sets. In turn, you want to avoid having just one, concrete resume and instead have the ability to adjust your resume as needed for each specific position. It can be difficult to try and remember everything you have achieved, especially as your years of experience start to add up! Just keep a generic Word **master document** with literally everything you have ever done and/or accomplished. Then, when it comes time to apply for a position, you can create a new document by cutting/pasting the appropriate information into a shorter, concise resume and you do not have to try and remember items from years ago. If pursuing a career in education, your employer may request a **curriculum vitae** or CV. The difference is a CV is a longer document that details all relevant experience throughout your career. All the more reason to maintain a master document.

© marekuliasz/Shutterstock.com

Before you start compiling your resume, think about your "brand" as a person. With all the digital avenues available, it is important to think about your image and how you want to be perceived by others who view your information. Frankel (2016) included several important steps including creating a professional email address, keeping social media set to private, using online resume sites such as LinkedIn, and even doing a simple web search of your name to see what appears. Having a professional email address is a great place to start your brand. Keep it simple – first name.last name@gmail.com. All other professional web media should also keep a consistent tag, so it is clear to the audience who they are contacting. Although your social media pages may be set to private, it does not mean that potential employers cannot access the information. Ask yourself a simple question when posting – what would someone think about your post/pictures? If it is potentially negative, or you are not sure, better be safe than sorry.

Now that you have your brand in order, it is time to create your resume. Think about the three C's – clean, concise, captivating.

Keep It Clean

"Clean" refers to several different aspects when creating your resume. The first item to consider is your format. When researching about how to write an effective resume, you will find thousands of different templates – the good, the bad, and the ugly. Here are a few format examples to start our conversation:

The first image is your traditional format, which many employers prefer. Although the others may appear more modern, remember who your audience is! This is a great sample if you are looking for a good guide on how to format your resume, the types of headings you might include, etc. The second example has a lot of bulleted lists, but no explanation. In addition, you will see the different "skills" sections include star ratings (4/5 stars with computer skills). Who determined the individual was 4/5 stars? What type of organization implements an evaluation system using stars? We will discuss how much depth to include in a resume later in the chapter. The final sample is definitely "unique." There are pictures, colors, and no clear order of information to follow. Keep your information clear and easy to find – Remember if your resume is judged within 10 seconds you do not want the reader wasting time looking for specific details.

Example 1

NAME SURNAME
P R O F E S S I O N A L   T I T L E

LOCATION: CITY, STATE
PHONE: (012) 444-5555
E-MAIL: NAME@SERVER.COM

OBJECTIVE:

Lorem ipsum dolor sit amet, consectetur adipiscing elit. Maecenas tortor dolor, pulvinar eget.

QUALIFICATION:

7 years experience as a aestibulum dignissim, sem sit amet aliquet varius
5 years experience of phasellus rhoncus diam et libero luctus egestas
4 years experience of fusce non tortor quam, ac viverra odio
7 years experience as a class aptent taciti sociosqu ad litora torquent per conubia nostra
3 years experience with etiam vitae interdum dolor

PROFESSIONAL EXPERIENCE:

CURRENT POSITION, CURRENT COMPANY   **2006 - PRESENT**

- Lorem ipsum dolor sit amet, consectetur adipiscing elit. Maecenas tortor dolor, pulvinar eget fermentum sed, convallis dignissim quam. Nulla eu est commodo leo porttitor consectetur. Aliquam vestibulum erat vitae arcu tristique quis ullamcorper lectus placerat.
- Vestibulum dignissim, sem sit amet aliquet varius, diam nulla malesuada arcu, aliquam lacinia arcu tortor quis ligula. Nulla fringilla metus ut lorem luctus ut iaculis erat tempor. Sed ornare fringilla nibh in aliquam. Lorem ipsum dolor sit amet, consectetur adipiscing elit. Phasellus rhoncus diam et libero luctus egestas.
- Quisque tristique pharetra leo eget imperdiet. Mauris dictum tortor quis turpis luctus fringilla. Vivamus varius massa accumsan turpis bibendum dictum. Fusce non tortor quam, ac viverra odio.
- Class aptent taciti sociosqu ad litora torquent per conubia nostra, per inceptos himenaeos. Quisque et tempor sapien.
- Morbi ut euismod velit. Curabitur rutrum turpis a augue pharetra sodales. Etiam vitae interdum dolor.
- Mauris eros felis, gravida vitae euismod ut, ultricies eu turpis.
- Fusce non tortor quam, ac viverra odio.

PREVIOUS POSITION, PREVIOUS COMPANY   **2003 - 2006**

- Duis et justo odio, et eleifend augue. Vestibulum ante ipsum primis in faucibus orci luctus et ultrices posuere cubilia.
- Proin dictum, dui id adipiscing consectetur, tortor lacus pulvinar risus, vitae vestibulum justo mi ac justo.
- Nullam ac suscipit ipsum. Nulla suscipit nisi ligula. Nam in ligula eget erat tempor aliquet. In a pharetra metus. Aliquam tristique quam a est tempus fringilla. Sed consectetur libero sit amet magna pulvinar consequat.
- Aenean rutrum ante id arcu tincidunt id vehicula arcu imperdiet. Praesent sollicitudin nisi et nibh faucibus vitae sagittis quam porttitor. Quisque pellentesque, lectus in blandit varius, nisl erat venenatis dolor.

OLDER POSITION, PLACE OF WORK IN THE PAST   **2002 - 2003**

- Aenean suscipit neque at nisl mollis posuere. Suspendisse interdum tincidunt leo ac consequat.
- Quisque felis dui, sollicitudin in lobortis sed, molestie a diam. Vestibulum semper elit non dolor varius posuere. Cras vehicula molestie suscipit. Morbi ullamcorper arcu ac ligula dapibus sollicitudin.

JUNIOR POSITION, FIRST JOB   **1994 - 2001**

- Fusce vehicula imperdiet ante eu adipiscing. Donec quam leo, fermentum pretium laoreet sit amet, vehicula in nulla. Pellentesque habitant morbi tristique senectus et netus et malesuada fames ac turpis egestas.
- Praesent diam mauris, dictum a tempus ac, faucibus consectetur leo.
- Vestibulum id elit tellus, fermentum hendrerit justo. Mauris nisi ipsum, ultricies non sodales vel, posuere quis tortor.
- Mauris metus tellus, consequat eu dignissim eu, feugiat in metus. Cras id ipsum a sem scelerisque blandit at aliquam eros. Praesent odio urna, dignissim eu malesuada dictum, feugiat ut lectus. Nunc et mi lorem.

EDUCATION:

- Nam in ligula eget erat tempor aliquet. In a pharetra metus.
- Sed consectetur libero sit amet magna pulvinar consequat.
- Aenean rutrum ante id arcu tincidunt id vehicula arcu imperdiet.

Example 2

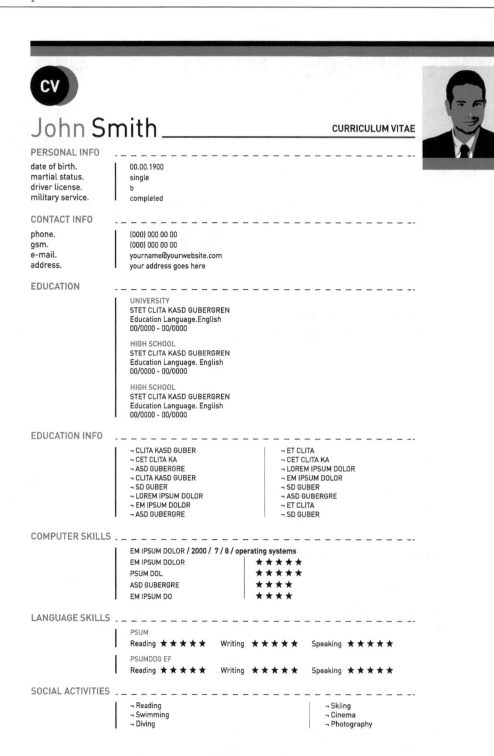

Example 3

Thankfully, there is more than one way to display your information correctly; however, you want to avoid some common pitfalls.

1. No matter which resume format you select, the very top of the document will include your name, contact information, and possibly an Objective Statement or Job Summary. Again, keep information clean and easy to read. Just because a specific font looks "pretty" does not mean it is the best choice. With your name, also include if you go by something different by colleagues or peers. For example, if you go by your middle name, you want to let the reviewer know that right away (especially when they call your references). So, if your name was Albert Markus Jones, and you go by Markus, you have some options for your resume. You could go with A. Markus Jones or Albert "Markus" Jones to indicate you answer to your middle name.

   Contact information "should" be self-explanatory; however, we often see errors in submissions in this area too. Information should include your mailing address, city, state, zip code, phone number, and email address.

   Full Mailing Address
   City, State, ZIP
   Cell - (xxx) xxx-xxxx
   Email - first name.last name@gmail.com

© Rawpixel.com/Shutterstock.com

The mailing address is often used to send additional information, letters to notify the position was filled, etc., so it is important you provide accurate personal information so an employer may contact you. Just because you were not hired this time does not mean you would not be considered for a future position. With your phone number, be sure to include dashes or periods to break up the number so it is easy to read. Ten numbers crammed together can be difficult for the reader to view easily. We already discussed creating a professional email address to fit your "brand" as an individual.

Also, some resume templates may have a place to add your picture like Examples #2 and #3 above. Granted some careers require a headshot (think about an actor submitting a resume for an audition). However, most jobs do not need a profile picture so better to leave that off of a resume. Although inappropriate (and potentially illegal) a reviewer make make a snap judgement based on your image. Hopefully, they will have a chance to meet you face-to-face and get a better picture of who you are when you land an interview!

The **Objective Statement** or **Job Summary** falls directly beneath the contact information and answers the question – "What are you applying for?" Think of the statement/summary as a thesis statement for your presentation. Sum up your expectations and desires in one to two sentences. "I want a position working in your organization" does not tell the reader WHAT position you are seeking. Often businesses are hiring multiple positions simultaneously, paperwork can get shuffled, and you want to be sure your application goes into the correct hands. In addition, the statement is the first chance the employer has to see your writing style, your passion for the field, and your desire immediately when reviewing your document. Start off with a good first impression!

2. All of your information needs to be easy to read and go through quickly. Remember that the average time spent looking at a resume is 10 seconds, so you do not want the reader to be fighting to find information. Use a readable typeface, have clear headings/breakdown of information, and use the same format throughout the entire document (do not change fonts, colors, spacing, bullets, etc.). Keep everything consistent. Some common headings include education, employment, skills, etc. Remember when you select different resume formats, you do not have to keep the headings suggested. If you do not have anything to include under a heading then delete it, do not put "None" underneath! Even better, change the heading to something you need to include. Keep in mind you do not have to use a pre-made template. Feel free to create your own design, select appropriate headings, etc. to ensure you highlight the information you believe is important. Plus, it could make your resume stand out from all of the other applicants who used the first template they found online!

© dizain/Shutterstock.com

3. Edit your resume (and have someone else review it as well). CareerBuilder surveyed hiring managers and human resource employers to discover the most common mistakes that would automatically dismiss a candidate. A resume that had typos was the number one response with 58%. How embarrassing would it be to describe yourself as detail-oriented, but have spelling errors within the document?

Keep It Concise

You want to keep your resume to one page in length (maybe two pages if printed front to back). If you do use the back of your document, you need to fill up the entire page, and make sure the most relevant information is on the front (if two-sided). The back may never be reviewed! Resumes are short and sweet, designed to highlight specific jobs, education, and skills, versus a curriculum vitae that would cover your entire work history. Although the resume is condensed, you do not want to keep it too short where you are only turning in bullet points and no details about your experiences. You need to fill up that page with information about you. Remember you are trying to sell yourself to a potential employer – only half of a page will not work!

1. List only relevant jobs and skills.

   We often work at a variety of jobs before landing the "dream job" and try to cram everywhere we worked into a one-page resume. Pick out the jobs and experiences you had that directly relate to the position you are seeking and remove the rest. However, you may need to keep some of those other work experiences if you need to fill up the page.

   Frequently we are asked the question, "What if I have only worked part-time jobs up to this point?" Do not worry; we all started somewhere and had those "survival" jobs in the meantime to pay the bills. Yes, you want to include those positions even if you do not see the connection to the dream job. However, what skills did you gain, and/or what did you learn at those jobs that will help with your future career? Those are the connections you want to highlight on a resume. If you ran the cash register at a store, then you probably gained experience in handling money, working with customers, resolving customer complaints, etc. Describe what you learned at those positions that prepared you for the position you want now. Do not just list tasks completed at the job - focus on the skills/abilities learned at that workplace.

2. Avoid paragraphs. Yes, you will have to provide some detail and explanation about things you have accomplished, but you do not submit a biography of your entire life. Remember you want to keep your resume clean so information needs to be easy to consume quickly. However, you do not just want a bulleted list of tasks completed at work either. It is a balance between key words and full paragraphs to inform the employer of your skill sets.

3. Stay focused on the job you are applying for. Be sure that the items you list have a connection to the position. Listing hobbies or achievements such as being an all-district quarterback, voted homecoming queen are great and all, but what in the world does that have to do with seeking a position in finance? Refer back to Resume Example #2. At the bottom the candidate includes social activities such as swimming, photography, and skiing. How is this information relevant to the job you are seeking? Make sure there is a reason to list certain information and avoid irrelevant facts. Remember you only have one page, so make the most of it!

© doomu/Shutterstock.com

© Lucky Business/Shutterstock.com

Captivate Your Audience

Realize the hiring committee is going through multiple resumes trying to narrow down whom they want to call in for an interview. What is going to make you stand out compared with all of the other "hard-working, motivated, team players" in the stack? An article posted on Monster highlights several items to consider when working to catch someone's eye.

© ESB Professional/Shutterstock.com

1. Obviously, it is necessary to talk about previous jobs and experiences, but "how" you talk about them makes all the difference. Instead of just covering the tasks at the job, what did you actually accomplish in the workplace? Were you responsible for specific duties? What happened when the job was completed? Did your boss trust you with additional responsibilities or projects?

2. A resume should not just be a summary of your past. Think about your wording as how your jobs and experiences prepared you for the future job you want. Oftentimes, we work "jobs" just to pay the bills as we go through school or gain training for the careers we really want. What did you learn at those jobs that will apply to your career? If you worked in the service industry, you learned how to work in a fast-paced environment. In retail, dealing with angry customers prepared you for conflict management. What did you gain working at those jobs that make you the perfect candidate for this position? That is what people want to know.

3. Avoid common buzzwords. Adams (2014) compiled a great list of words on Forbes.com to avoid using as well as words to include when describing yourself. Here are a few from the list below:

Words to Avoid	Words to Use
Best of Breed	Achieved
Go-Getter	Improved
Think Outside the Box	Resolved
Synergy	Created
Go-To Person	Launched
Team Player	Trained
Hard Worker	Negotiated
Detail-Oriented	Managed

So why avoid words on the list? Two words: Prove it! "How" are you a hard worker? Describe being a go-to person. Give an example of when you thought outside of the box. This goes back to point number one. Be specific about what you accomplished, achieved, or learned at your previous jobs. Describing yourself as a "go-getter" does not tell the reader what you were a go-getter doing in the organization. Only stating you are "detailed oriented" does not accurately describe how you served as an editor for your boss' letters and public announcements. Use active words to describe what really happened in previous situations: negotiated, resolved, trained, etc. That helps paint a picture of the type of employee you will be for their organization.

The last item you might include on your resume is the line "References Available Upon Request". Do not list your references and/or their contact information directly on your resume. Although references are commonly required, they are included either directly on the job application or, if not, include them on a separate sheet of paper. References are viewed as "filler" on a resume, as though you did not have enough to say about yourself so you included your references to fill up the page so it was not so empty! When creating your references page, use the same format as your resume with the heading, font, etc. so it looks identical, and then list your references (generally 3–5 people) below. Provide their name, their position, and contact information for individuals to reach out and ask them questions. Use current/former bosses, colleagues, professors, etc. as your references – never family members! Also be sure to ask your references permission to list them BEFORE submitting your application. You want to be sure they have a heads-up that they might be contacted.

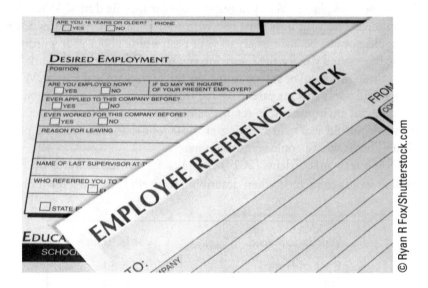

© Ryan R Fox/Shutterstock.com

Remember there is more than one way to appropriately format your document. Keep in mind the tips mentioned above and make the most of out the space on the page. It is always easier to see errors in the examples versus looking at our own work, so take the time to really edit your document!

Cover Letters

With your resume ready to go, now it is time to prepare the **cover letter**, the introduction to who you are, and what position you are seeking. Just like with the resume, you want to keep your cover letter brief. The employer will see all of the important details highlighted within your resume. The point of the cover letter is to express what position you are interested in and explain "why" you are interested and seeking an interview while keeping a conversational tone (Akpan & Notar, 2012). Once again, editing, spelling, and format are important, so keep consistent with how you designed your resume.

© Fazakas Mihaly/Shutterstock.com

The cover letter is a chance to really sell yourself! Yes, you have an objective statement on your resume and all of your previous work experience, but that does not express your passion for the position you want. First, you want to attend to the information included in the original job announcement. Are there certain skills and qualifications the candidate needs to have? Are there any preferred skills you also possess? Go through the job posting and pick out all of the criteria and expectations they want. That list of criteria needs to be addressed within your cover letter. Along with the basic job requirements, you NEED to express your desire for the position. A good cover letter can trump not having years of experience in the field. A potential candidate who shows true passion for the job, is hungry to learn more, and shows enthusiasm and eagerness to get to work can be impressive to a hiring committee. Sell who you are and why you would be the best fit for the job. We have also included a sample cover letter below. For additional help, check out the chapter concerning good writing in business on formatting your resumes and cover letters.

Sample Cover Letter

Month Day, Year

Your Name
Address
City, State Zip
Email Address
Members of the Search Committee
Organization, Location
Organization Contact Email Address

Dear communication colleagues and members of the search committee:

It is with great excitement I submit my materials for consideration of the opportunity: Tenure-track position in Media Studies. I have no doubt you will receive a multitude of qualified applicants for this position. To that end, I will highlight below my experiences as a teacher-scholar in order to demonstrate the breadth and depth of my career so the committee can better understand my portfolio.

Based on the job description in the Chronicle, it appears this opportunity needs a professor who can teach various courses in the media arts and communication theory. I studied for my terminal master's degree in Marketing Management Communication at Generic University. Throughout that program our course work encompassed many of the aspects of the visual media discipline yet rooted it in traditional critical and cultural approaches of analysis using communication theory. For example, my final project/thesis was a rhetorical analysis including specific rhetorical themes to analyze media texts.

That educational experience offered me the opportunity to work in industry helping consult on Web and video projects for my state and beyond. After my work in industry in XXX I moved to XXX for a full-time appointment as the Coordinator of Communication. In our Business Communication classes we have used critical analysis to analyze business materials, TED Talks, and other popular culture media that students see—but often have not thought deeply about. Additionally, this appointment has given me the opportunity to lead nine education study abroad courses.

Special topics courses such as the *Communication Model and Italy* have infused elements of advanced media theory, multimedia production, visual communication and distinct features of proper writing. In the business communication honors courses I teach, students create a non-profit organization and pitch it to actual community members for possible funding and/or networking. In these classes I teach a full communications campaign founded in an integrated marketing approach: collateral, social media and visual media; and website design and creation. Students use the campaign to attract the community members they wish to evaluate their final non-profit pitches for their final projects.

It is my hope that my materials demonstrate a "good-fit" for me with XXX Organization and its mission. I firmly believe in what the institution is doing and have visited the campus and its surrounding areas many times. If there are any questions about my credentials or experience please let me know so I may provide further explanation. I would be honored to discuss this opportunity further.

Respectfully,

Interviewing

So, you submitted the resume, and bingo, you have been called in for an interview. Time to prepare for the next step. Through this section of the chapter, we will cover each part of the interview process from arriving to the interview site to what happens after the interview is all said and done.

Sometimes with interviews, you may have the option of what time you will come in to meet with the person and/or committee. If possible, try to have a morning time slot versus after lunch or at the end of the day. We are not saying that afternoon people do not get hired, but you may have to work harder to keep their attention after a long day of interviews. Plus, if you are in the morning, you could be the individual that "sets the tone" or that everyone compares future candidates against. It is great if you stick in their mind (for a good reason)! Do not worry if you are scheduled for an afternoon time frame. It just means you have the opportunity to be the "closer" candidate the committee has been waiting to see all day!

First and foremost, you NEVER want to be late to an interview. Give yourself plenty of time to arrive at the interview early. Personally, we subscribe to the "if you're on time, you're late – if you're 10 minutes early, you're on time". If you are unsure about where you are going, parking, traffic, etc., it might be a good idea to do a test run to the location beforehand so you are not lost or panicky on the day of your interview. You have enough to think about already! The interview process begins as soon as you set foot on site. We worked with an individual who would watch as candidates parked in visitor parking to see what vehicle they drove. To take it a step farther, they would go out to their car and peer in the windows. Creepy yes, but what information could people determine about you by looking in your car? Are you neat and organized? Do you eat fast food all of the time? Do you have a car seat and/or toys in the back? Might go ahead and clean up all aspects of yourself before an interview, including your vehicle in case a creepy person works there!

In addition, interview committees often schedule interviews back to back to try and avoid disrupting the committee members' schedules too much and avoid too much time between potential candidates. If the person interviewing before you wraps up early, it gives the committee a chance to continue immediately with the interviewing process, which is often appreciated. In addition, it gives you a chance to chat with

whoever might be in the waiting area (administrative assistants, work study students, etc.). Those individuals are the gatekeepers. Assistants keep offices running, so be sure to treat them with respect – you are interviewing with them as well. Do not think how you act in the waiting room is not reported to the hiring committee! Office staff frequently can guess which person is hired simply by their actions (or lack thereof) while waiting.

Be sure to bring a portfolio, notepad, and a pen with you to your interview. You may want to take notes over important details that are discussed by the

© djile/Shutterstock.com

committee. In addition, if you are asked a question that has two or more parts you need to address it is good to write down the question to ensure you answer all aspects and not forget to answer a section of the question! Also bring copies of your resume and a list of references. Granted the committee will have already reviewed your information, but it is good to have copies on hand just in case. Most importantly, have questions prepared that you would like to ask the interviewer(s). Interviews often end with the "Do you have any questions for us?" DO NOT ask about the pay rate or vacation time! (Those questions come later once they have offered you the position.) You want to have thoughtful questions for the group. "What should be my top priorities in the first 90 days?" "How does the company measure success?" "How long have YOU been with the company?" Of course, you will also want to know when you can expect to hear about whether you have been hired or not. The point is to show that you are truly interested in this position.

There is a saying that we never have a second chance to make a good first impression. That is very true when it comes to entering an interview situation. A great concept to think about with each aspect of interviewing and first impressions is the 10 x 10 x 10 approach. You are immediately judged from 10 feet away, from 10 inches away, and the first 10 words out of your mouth.

10 feet away – Entering the Room – Realize that the interviewer and interview committee are judging you the first moment they lay eyes on you. They are trying to figure out who you are, what you will bring to the organization, if you are someone they could see working with day in and day out, etc. Be sure to dress for the part. A good rule of thumb is to dress one step above whatever the "normal" attire is for that position/organization. If the dress code is jeans and a shirt, then go khakis and polo. If it is business casual, then go dress shirt and tie, and so on. Just because you might get to wear scrubs everyday does not mean that is appropriate for an interview. Whatever attire you need to wear, be sure that you are polished. Clothes need to be ironed, shoes shined, etc. If you do not have appropriate attire (and cannot afford expensive clothing), check out your local thrift and consignment stores. Often you will find name brand clothing that will work perfectly for an interview situation, and you would not have to spend a lot of money. When it comes to your appearance, make sure that hair is trimmed and neatly groomed. Avoid crazy hairstyles, hair colors, and anything that may be a distraction from showing the interview committee what an asset you truly are. Wear jewelry in moderation, avoiding large, flashy, and/or items that jingle every time you move. Ladies, you need to wear makeup. Again, nothing extreme. Each aspect of your appearance comes together to tell a story about who you are and how seriously you feel about this job opportunity.

10 inches away – You have entered the space, now it is time to make the rounds. Introduce yourself to every person in the room. The "10 inches away" refers to the up-close moments with the interviewer(s). Practice your handshake! We know it sounds awkward, but you want to have a strong handshake and not one that crushes the other person's hand. While introducing yourself, try to remember everyone's names so you can refer to them directly during the interview process. This can be difficult (especially with a large interview committee), but it can help you score points. Maintain eye contact with each person as you shake their hand and learn their name. That will also help you connect names to faces as you go through the process.

10 words out of your mouth – Interviews are typically an impromptu style delivery – you do not know what the interviewer is going to ask you specifically. However, you can bet on some questions (in one form or another) being asked. Think about it—What are the first things you usually say in each interview? What is the first question most interviews begin with? "So tell us a little about yourself. . ."

That's one answer you should already have prepped and ready to go. It is not an opening for you to tell your entire life story. Instead, you should have a prepared, confident, short summation about who you are, your education, and a brief explanation of how you came to apply for this position. You will have plenty of opportunity to explain about all of your experiences and skills through the interview process. (Remember this is usually just the opening question!) The interviewers will have a set of questions to go through and dive into the details, so do not try to share it all up front. You will get your opportunity! At the end of the interview, if you feel there is additional information you need to share about yourself, be sure to include that in your time to ask questions as a closing summary about yourself and why you would be a great fit for the position.

Online Interviews

With today's technology, we do not have to travel across the state, country, or even the world to interview for a position. Now, we have the ability to meet with a hiring committee right at our fingertips. Even before the pandemic, many organizations were using online interviews for a first round screening of candidates (Edwards, 2020). According to USA Today (2020), "... a Forbes article indicates that 89% of employers now are moving towards virtual interviews" (p. 3). The point is to be prepared to conduct your interview no matter the format. Despite the ease of interviewing online, there are some important factors to remember when preparing to interview through this format. Thankfully, some of the same rules discussed previously apply to prepare for an online interview that you would follow if conducting the interview in person. Here are a few more items to consider for the online interview.

1. Be on Time/Check Your Technology. It is the same thought process as a live interview. You do not want to keep a group of people waiting. No matter what program or software you are using, be sure to do a test run of your microphone, the camera, etc. so you are not surprised the day of the interview. Be sure to select a location with reliable internet access as well! As a backup, have the employer's contact information handy if something should occur and you lose your connection. Realize you are not alone if you do not have reliable technology or internet access. Sauers (2021) noted, "an estimated 19 million Americans-or 6% of the population-still lack access to fixed broadband service at threshold speeds" (p. 18). If this is a concern, check for available spaces at your local libraries (see #2 below about surroundings).

2. Be Aware of Surroundings. Pick a location to conduct your interview where you will not be inter-rupted. Remember, you want to be the focus during the entire interview process. You do not want your committee distracted by items in the background. Remember the creepy guy looking in cars in the face-to-face interview described earlier? Individuals will try to figure out what books are on the shelf behind you, are there children's toys on the floor, what pictures are on the walls, etc. Make sure there is not anything to draw their attention away. Consider using a virtual background that is simple or blurs everything behind you. If the technology does not have a background option, hang a white sheet or sit in front of a plain wall, and ensure you have good lighting so that your audience can easily see you (Brettschneider, 2020).

   The picture below actually occurred during job interviews. It is amazing how many pets make an appearance during an online interview or meeting. The session turns into a game of "Find the Kitty" instead of a serious conversation about the candidate! Make sure to shut doors and keep your animals out of the situation. If that is not possible in your home (as many animals rule the house), then perhaps find a different location so you are not distracted. Sauers (2021) discussed how many community libraries installed separate small rooms and/or labs for individuals to use to limit distractions and have reliable technology available.

© garetsworkshop/Shutterstock.com

3. Dress the Part. I know you may be thinking, "Why would I dress up for an online or phone interview?" There is something to be said about wearing your "interview clothes" that helps put you in the mindset of the interview process. Remember you are still making a first impression to the hiring committee and you do not want to be caught (literally) in your pajama bottoms, if you suddenly shift or move the wrong way during your interview.

© Maridav/Shutterstock.com

4. Keep your notes and resume handy. It is ok to have your notes on your screen or on your desk to refer back to when asked a question. However, it is important that you do not read to the interviewers! Just have a few bullet points, some examples you might want to share, or skills you want to highlight during the course of the interview. You do not want to have the "Oh, I should have said X" moment after the interview is over.

5. Keep eye contact with the camera (audience). It is extremely difficult to look at the actual camera instead of your screen with yourself on it. Remember the camera is your audience! Referring back to the # 1 tip, check your technology prior to the session to make sure you are clearly visible so you do not have to check your own performance while trying to answer interview questions.

Video Interviews/Video Resume

Some organizations may ask you to record yourself and submit a video interview along with your resume and initial application. Researchers also refer to this as a 'video resume.' There are two main types of video resumes that occur. First, the employer may ask for a generic, summary video of yourself explaining who you are and a basic breakdown of your skill sets. Often the video is no longer than five minutes in length. The idea is for the hiring team to initially learn who you are, what position you are seeking, and why you believe you are the best fit for the job (remember they are receiving multiple applications to review). You should NOT read through your paper resume – you probably submitted that document along with the video. The goal is to highlight and explain specific examples, demonstrate your passion for the field, and convince the organization to move you to the next round of interviews.

The second type of Video Resume involves answering specific questions provided by the employer. (Equivalent to the scripted interview described below.) With a scripted video, the hiring committee can compare answers with other candidates to narrow down the applicant pool. Similar to the summary video, you will have a limited amount of time to answer the provided questions, and you should NOT read the answers you prepared to the questions. Your delivery and presentation style matter just as much (sometimes more) than the answers to the questions themselves. Here are some important suggestions to keep in mind if you need to prepare a video resume.

1. Quality counts. Just like with a live online interview, it is just as important to check your background, how you present yourself, and ensure the video is easy to view. Check the lighting, sound, orientation, etc. of your video before you submit! If the committee cannot hear/see you, the video is sideways, etc. it does not make a positive first impression and will probably keep you from moving to the next round of interviewing.
2. Answer questions professionally and thoroughly. If asked a yes/no question, be sure to answer 'why' your answer is yes or no. Give some examples, provide detail, and explain your answer.
3. Try to develop a rapport with the audience. Yes, we understand the difficulty in this step because you do not have a live audience. However, this video is a chance to show your personality, how you communicate, body language, etc. so it is important to consider the nonverbal aspects of your delivery as well as answering the questions.
4. Practice and Do More than One Take! The great thing about a video resume is that you have more than one chance to create a great video. The bad thing is that the hiring committee also knows you had more than one opportunity to get it right! You are going to mess up, fumble words, get distracted, etc. However, unlike a live moment, you have the chance to delete and start again. Take advantage of the ability to rerecord your video because your competition has the same chance as you to perfect the recording.

Interview Formats

There are two main types of interview formats: scripted and unscripted. A **scripted** format has the interviewer ask the same set of questions to each person being interviewed. One pro to a scripted interview is that it allows the interviewers to compare answers from one candidate to the next since each person was asked the exact same questions; however, it does not allow for much flexibility and veering away from the planned questions. The **unscripted** format can literally be whatever question comes to an interviewer's mind that they want to ask! Often, this format occurs in a one-on-one interview situation. The pro is that the interviewer can ask follow-up questions and go down a rabbit hole of different information with each individual. The difficult part becomes tracking the information that was asked and how each person answered the questions. Often times, interviewees experience a mix of both the scripted/unscripted formats. The committee may have a plan of questions ready to go, but it does not mean they cannot ask follow-up questions or for clarification on an answer.

Types of Interview Questions

There are three main types of questions commonly asked in interviews: general, behavioral, and situational. The good thing is that you can easily find sample questions online and practice what you might answer if asked during an interview.

General Questions are used to investigate the applicant's beliefs, goals, and motivations. It gives the candidate the opportunity to share details about their life/career, important moments they want to emphasize, and a chance to present a more personal side to who they are as a person. Here are some sample general questions:

Sample Questions	Sample Answers
Tell us about yourself.	Almost always the first question asked in any interview! Have a short summary prepared (refer back to what we mentioned earlier with the "first 10 words out of your mouth.")
Why did you choose your major/this career field?	Why are you passionate about this job? (your answer should not be salary based!)
What do you see yourself in five years?	The answer is to better understand where you see yourself and how you would like to grow and/or move up within the company. Never that you want to work somewhere else!
Tell us about one of you proudest accomplishments.	This does not have to be an award or formal recognition. Maybe your proudest accomplishment is earning a B in a class that is not your strongest subject, but you worked hard, went to tutoring, etc. and were successful.

Behavioral Questions ask the candidate to recall or describe a past experience and then detail how they responded to the situation. Some sample Behavioral Questions include:

Sample Questions

Give an example of how you worked effectively under pressure.
What do you do when your schedule is interrupted? Give an example of how you handle it.
Tell us about a goal you achieved and how you accomplished it.
How would you respond to a request to complete a task that you have never done before?

The **STAR approach** is a great way to manage answering behavioral questions to ensure you discuss each part of the process and the role you played in handling the situation.

- **S**ituation description
- **T**asks that needed to be done
- **A**ction(s) you took
- **R**esults you achieved

Use one of the sample questions above and create an answer including each of the four steps. With the first question, describe a stressful situation at work or school that caused added pressure to you and/or your team. Describe brainstorming solutions and possibly working with others to determine how to fix the problem and identifying tasks. With the Actions step, it is absolutely ok to say that you consulted your boss/supervisor for help and guidance on the situation. It can be a red flag if an individual attempts to solve a problem (especially major conflicts) on their own! Finally, with the results, it is expected to explain what worked and what failed in your attempt to fix the problem. If something did not work out the way you predicted, what did you learn from the process for the next time a similar incident occurs?

Situational Questions provide the candidate with a scenario (instead of the candidate coming up with their own example) and ask how s/he would respond. Situational questions are "stress questions" to see how you will react under pressure, can you be creative in your answers, do you understand standard policies/procedures, etc.

Sample Questions

What would you do if you were assigned to work on a project with a co-worker but the two of you cannot agree on how to proceed?
As a leader, you will have to introduce new topics and processes to your team. How would you react if your team resisted a new idea you introduced? What if only a few team members resist?
As you are closing up for the day, you notice one of your co-workers take money from the cash register. How would you handle the situation?
A customer contacts your boss to report that you were rude in answering their questions and unwilling to help solve their problem. What is your response to your supervisor?

No matter which interview format is used or the types of questions asked, it is important to realize that some questions cannot be asked and are considered illegal. Business Insider presented, "State and federal laws make discrimination based on certain protected categories, such as national origin, citizenship, age, marital status, disabilities, arrest and conviction record, military discharge status, race, gender, or pregnancy status, illegal. Any question that asks a candidate to reveal information about such topics without the question having a job related basis will violate the various state and federal discrimination laws," Lori Adelson, a labor and employment attorney and partner with law firm Arnstein & Lehr, tells Business Insider. There may be situations in which the illegal question needs to be asked because of the job requirements; however, you have to be VERY sure that you are not violating any laws.

So, what are your options if you are asked an illegal question? First rule: Never lie. Even if the question is not supposed to be asked, two wrongs do not make a right. You can politely decline to answer the question. Could this cost you the job? Possibly. However, A) you might not want to work for an organization that makes those kinds of errors and B) declining you a job based on illegal questions is exactly why laws are in place to prevent such practices. There is always the "beat around the bush" approach. Say an interviewer asks, "Are you married with children?" ILLEGAL! An option to respond might be, "My family is very supportive of my career goals and know how much this job would mean to me." I did not tell you if I was married and/or had children. I just talked in general about my family. This way the interviewer has an answer to the question without revealing any specifics.

However if YOU, as the candidate, bring up information about your children, marriage, etc. in your answers, then you have opened the door for the hiring committee to ask follow-up questions about your answers which goes into rule number two: Leave out the drama!

Avoid bringing up personal issues, previous work conflicts, family troubles, etc. when in an interview setting. It is not a confessional – you do not need to tell all! If you left a previous job on bad terms, you do not want to "bash" former bosses/coworkers either. Some businesses and career fields are small. Everybody knows somebody who worked at that location. You might be talking negatively about someone's relative, so tread lightly.

Hopefully, this chapter provided some useful insights on interviewing, from creating your resumes and cover letters to going through the entire process. If you have not started collecting your information and job history you are behind! When that dream job is posted, you want to have everything ready to go to have the best chance of being hired. Practice sample interview questions and have confidence knowing that you did everything you could to earn the position.

REFERENCES

11 Common Interview Questions that are Actually Illegal. (n.d.). Retrieved January 16 2017, from http://www.businessinsider.com/11-illegal-interview-questions-2013-7

Akpan, J. & Notar, C. E. (2012). How to write a professional knockout resume to differentiate yourself. *College Student Journal, 46*(4), 880–891.

Barden, D. M.(2021). Are We Talking Too Much in Video Interviews? *Chronicle of Higher Education, 67*(15).

Brettschneider, K. (2020). How to Ace the Virtual Interview. *Chronicle of Higher Education, 66*(28).

CareerBuilder Releases Study of Common and Not-So-Common Resume Mistakes That Can Cost You the Job (2013). Retrieved January 12 2017, from http://www.careerbuilder.com/share/aboutus/pressreleasesdetail.aspx?sd =9%2f11%2f2013&siteid=cbpr&sc_cmp1=cb_pr780_&id=pr780&ed=12%2f31%2f2013.http://www. forbes.com/sites/susanadams/2014/03/17/the-best-and-worst-words-to-use-on-your-resume/#2c97954633e4

Challenges of the Video Job Interview. (2020). *USA Today, 149*(2903), 3.

Edwards, B. T. (2020). End the In-Person Job Interview. *Chronicle of Higher Education, 67*(5).

Frankel, C. (2016). Resume writing in the digital age. *Veterinary Team Brief, 4*(4), 18–21. https://www.monster.com/career-advice/article/resume-mistakes-that-will-cost-you-the-job.

Hamilton, H. (n.d.). *5 Resume Mistakes that Will Cost You the Job.* Retrieved January 10, 2017 from https:// www.monster.com/career-advice/article/resume-mistakes-that-will-cost-you-the-job

Kimbrel, L. (2021). The impact of virtual employment interviews on the teacher hiring process. *Administrative Issues Journal: Connecting Education, Practice, and Research, 11*(1), 1-16.

Sauers, M. (2021). Acing the Interview. Tech library assists locals in finding jobs by providing access to digital tools. *Trends Spotlight, 4*(12), 18–19.

Chapter

14 Listening and Meetings

This chapter examines a situation that most employees dread. That awful sentence, "Let's call a meeting." Although meetings can serve an important purpose, we have all been through that meeting where information could have been sent in an email. So how do we prepare purposeful meetings?

What behaviors are appropriate to enact? How do we carefully listen to the information disseminated? We hope the following chapter will answer those questions.

First, we need to understand the basic (although not easy) function of being an effective listener. Listening and hearing are NOT the same thing. Although you could be hearing the sounds coming at you, it does not mean you are processing the information. Active, engaged **listening** is defined as avoiding interruption, staying focused, avoiding evaluation, organizing information, and providing feedback (Jahromi, Tabatabaee, Abdar, & Rajabi, 2016). There are several steps that occur when making the effort to be a good listener.

Select – Selecting is what information is actually heard/taken in by the listener. We do not notice or acknowledge all of the sounds around us, so it focuses in on the information that is absorbed.

Attend – This is probably the most difficult step. This is giving the person speaking your complete, undivided attention while they are speaking.

Thanks to technology, the attention spans of humans keep shrinking. Watson (2015) reported, ". . .the average human attention span has fallen from 12 seconds in 2000, or around the time the mobile revolution began, to eight seconds."

Understand – We will talk about this step in-depth in a little while, but understanding is the processing of information and comprehending what the person is saying. We tend to shut down and stop trying to listen if we cannot understand what is discussed.

Remember – The Remember step can last as long as a few seconds to months later. It refers to the ability to retain information to recall at the appropriate time. Do you need to provide feedback in the moment, is the content something you need to perform a task when you get back to your office, or is it valuable information to store for a rainy day?

Respond – The final step is to provide some type of response to the individual, which could be verbal and/or nonverbal feedback. This includes a head nod to indicate you are paying attention, asking questions about the information presented, or taking notes.

Now that we understand the process of listening, everything will be communicated clearly right? Not quite. Although the procedure has defined steps, each of us has a different way we take in information and what catches our attention. This is known as our **listening style**, or our preferred way of understanding messages. Watson, Barker, and Weaver (1995) broke down listening styles into four different categories: people-oriented, action-oriented, content-oriented, and time-oriented. This is difficult for us as presenters because you may have all four types of listeners present in your audience, and you will need to address their needs/goals when they are listening to you.

People-Oriented Listeners – The people-oriented listening is interested in, you got it, the person speaking. Potentially, they may be more interested in the person versus the content presented. By default, the listener could become interested in the topic simply because of the

© SK Design/Shutterstock.com

© donskarpo/Shutterstock.com

person presenting the information. Some examples include celebrity endorsements or when the speaker includes their own personal stories while presenting.

Action-Oriented Listeners – The action-oriented listener is focused on finding the answer to a single question. What do you (the speaker) want? The action-oriented listener wants to "do something" based on information presented. They do not necessarily want all of the backstory, research, or "why" certain tasks need to be completed. They just want to know what to do after the speaker concludes their message.

Content-Oriented Listeners – This person is all about the message. The content-oriented listener wants the speaker to present a clear address that makes sense, includes facts to support their points, and not try to "sell" them on their perspective. They want the speaker to have a well-prepared and researched presentation.

Time-Oriented Listener – The "get to the point" listener. This type of audience member does not appreciate lots of detail or long, drawnout presentations. Realize if you are presenting during a meeting, there may be other items on the agenda. You cannot spend a great deal of time on your topic because the individuals have other business items to address. You want a concise presentation that hits the high points and concludes quickly.

Obstacles to Listening

No matter the efforts we put in to trying to being a good listener, we have multiple obstacles in our path that keep us from being successful. It goes back to our first chapter where we discussed the noise we experience, both as a speaker or audience member. When it comes to obstacles, we experience both external and internal distractions that may keep us from receiving a message. Let us examine the External Obstacles first.

1. **Message Overload** – Simply put, we have too much information to take in and retain. Think about how many classes you sit through in a row. For some of you, this may be two, three, even four classes of content. That is only part of your day! Add in all of your conversations with friends, family, bosses, coworkers, kids, etc. and it can feel extremely overwhelming.
2. **Message Complexity** – Imagine you are sitting in a meeting and your boss begins using a series of abbreviations to describe different organizations or processes to apply when you get back to your office. It may sound like alphabet soup! "I need HR to review FAFSA and FERPA guidelines with your department ASAP." If you do not understand what is communicated you are experiencing message complexity, which is information you do not understand or is over your head.
3. **Noise** – Back to our communication model, noise refers to those outside distractions that can keep us from receiving a message. Noise includes anything from someone coughing, clicking pens, phones beeping, traffic on the highway, etc.

Now that we understand the external obstacles, let us look at the internal obstacles that get in our way too!

"Hold my calls until I'm willing to listen."

1. Pre-occupation – You are taking a full load of classes, you go to work, you think about what to make for dinner, scheduling time for homework, making plans for the weekend and suddenly someone asks, "So what do you think?" You have no idea what the person said prior to that moment because you are distracted with your own thoughts. **Pre-occupation** is also referred to as "internal noise" or those thoughts and voices in your head that prevent us from being a good listener.
2. Prejudgment – Have you ever purchased tickets to attend a concert or hear someone speak and you were extremely excited to hear? It would not matter if the band or person did not perform at their

© Antonio Guillem/Shutterstock.com

best because you were looking forward to the event so much. The reverse is true too; you cannot stand a certain individual, and it would not matter if they had the most interesting presentation prepared because you already decided it would be terrible. **Prejudgment** is deciding you are willing/unwilling to listen before the information is even communicated.

3. Focusing on Emotionally Loaded Language – **Emotionally loaded language** refers to words or phrases that irritate us or "get under our skin." We do not like when people use them in their delivery and can make us uncomfortable (or even angry) when said. Often when a person uses loaded language, we shut down and do not want to hear any more from this person. Some examples include the use of profanity, pet/kid names (honey, sweetie, son, boy), or even phrases "Whatever. . . ." "let's take a selfie" etc. The problem is what may be "loaded" language for one audience member may not be an issue for another.

Despite our best efforts to be good listeners and overcome all of the different obstacles, we still struggle to be active in our listening approach and give the person speaking our full focus. There are many ways we act like we are listening, but are not in reality. These are known as the different forms of nonlistening.

Forms of Nonlistening

Pseudolistening – Pseudo means fake or false, so you are faking that you are listening. Nodding your head while someone is talking could be a type of response to the speaker, or it could be acting like you are listening while focused on something else. Another example could be the "uh huh" response when talking on the phone, but, in essence, you have no idea what the person has said.

Monopolizing – Another phrase to describe monopolizing would be story trumping. Think of a situation where you were telling a story and instead of the person listening asking questions and follow-up about your story, they respond with their own personal story. Monopolizing is focusing the communication back to you instead of actually listening to the person speaking.

Selective Listening – No, this is not gender specific or only applies to our children! Everyone is guilty of this one. Selective listening is where we focus on parts of the message and ignore the rest. However, it is not always a bad thing. Think about note taking in the classroom. You write down the information that you feel is pertinent and ignore the other facts that may not matter.

Defensive Listening – A defensive listener perceives personal attacks or criticism in a message where none was intended. They always believe you mean something other than what is actually said. For example, you tell someone "You look nice today." If they respond, "So what, I don't look nice everyday!?!". . .You might be in the presence of a defensive listener.

Ambushing – An ambusher listens carefully, but for the purpose of attacking the speaker. This is a great tactic in a debate. You are listening for the person to make a mistake or misquote something while presenting. Then, when it is your turn to respond, you point out their mistake over and over to decrease their credibility. Most of us will not encounter a debate situation, but we may have that friend who corrects our story as we are speaking or even corrects our grammar. That would be an everyday occurrence of ambushing.

Literal Listening – This form of nonlistening is becoming more prevalent with the advancements of technology. Literal listening is focusing only on the words used and ignoring the emotion and/or tone with the message. Think of emails and text messaging. You cannot "hear" how the person is communicating the message. Are they serious? Being sarcastic? Joking around? It can be easy to misinterpret a message when you only have the words on the screen.

Listening at Work

So far, we have covered the basics of listening, the obstacles that get in our way, and how we may act like we are listening, but not actually taking in any information. Now let us throw in another wrench in being a good listener – taking it to the workplace setting. There are several situations where being a good listener is imperative on the job. We will examine work meetings (both face-to-face and virtual), how to respond to others, and dealing with complaints.

Listening in Meetings

You are called to attend a meeting and immediately your reaction is "Well there goes two hours wasted from my day." Although we have covered presentations and tips for good speaking throughout the book, it is also important to discuss your role as an audience member. We will begin with some basic steps to keep in mind no matter what type of meeting you attend.

1. Avoid Prejudgment. We discussed the internal noise of judging a person before they begin to speak. The same theory applies to meetings. Yes, we have all been victims of the worthless meeting that could have been an email. However, do not judge that the meeting is a waste of your time before you even enter the space. If you walk into a meeting already in a bad mood, it will be hard to gain anything positive from the session. At least keep the hope that the person who organized the meeting has good intentions to run a smooth, organized conference with everyone present.

2. Set a Good Example. Remember you are not the only person in the room attending the meeting. Other people in attendance might include your colleagues, people that report to you, bosses and supervisors, etc. Employees look to you to set the tone for how to act and behave in situations. If you are in a bad mood, have expressed this is a waste of time, are playing games on your phone, etc., then why should they have to pay attention? In addition, your own bosses observe whether or not you are engaged in the meeting and making mental notes about how you act and participate in the session.

3. Write down information. Generally, meetings are called to include department heads, bosses, and key individuals within an organization that will disseminate information to others after the meeting concludes. If you have been called to the table, then it will be your job to make sure your team receives the information presented. You want to take good notes, write down important details, record any deadlines to complete tasks, and anything of importance that directly impacts your group.

4. Review/Clarify Before Leaving. It is ok to ask questions if you do not understand something in a meeting. More than likely someone else in the room may have the same question as you. Remember it is your job to explain the information to your team, so if you do not understand a concept or directive then you definitely need clarification before you lead your team down the wrong path. Nothing upsets employees more than having to redo work because of someone else's misunderstanding. However, there is an 'unspoken' courtesy to limit how many questions to ask in a meeting. (See Step # 5 below.)

5. Follow-up with Presenter. If you find that you have lots of questions or have questions that relate specifically to only your situation, then it is best to wait until after the presentation is over and approach the speaker directly. Audience members often hate the person that asks lots of questions, especially if they understand what is happening and are ready to leave. Let the speaker end the session, and then approach them with your list of questions for clarification before you leave the meeting.

LISTEN TO WHAT YOUR CLIENT WANTS

© Constantin Stanciu/Shutterstock.com

Running a Meeting

Now you are that dreaded person who called a group of people together in the workplace. You know how much you personally despise meetings that waste your time so you better be sure your meeting does not fall into that category too! The good news is you already have a head start after reviewing the chapters concerning organizing a speech, preparing a powerful message, and how to conduct quality research. All of these same techniques apply when you get ready to run a meeting. Even if you have a great message prepared, you need to ensure you run the actual meeting in an organized and concise format.

1. Review the Situation. Is a meeting absolutely necessary? Are there any other ways to either gather/give information to a set of people? If you believe it would be too confusing to try and disseminate data through email, online drives, etc. then a meeting may be your best option.

2. Who, What, and Where. Examine who needs to be present, what information will be covered, and where is the best location to host the meeting. Once you have identified who needs to attend the meeting, send out an invitation to find the best day/time that will fit with the majority of schedules. There are great (free) polling tools online to make this process easier. When you know the most opportune time, send out a message informing your audience of the day, time, and location of your meeting. Also, include how long you anticipate the meeting to last. Remember everyone is organizing their schedules to fit you in, so be respectful of their time. It is also great if you can include a short agenda or any information they need to review prior to the gathering.

3. Check your Location Again. Ensure that there are enough tables/chairs for everyone, that technology is available and working, and that the space is organized to fit your needs. Do you need everyone facing forward, is it a round table seminar, etc.? You do not want any additional surprises on the day of your meeting.

4. Arrive Early. You want to be ready to go so the meeting begins on time. Set up in your conference space with all of your materials prepared.

"Frankly, I don't remember why I called this meeting."

© Cartoon Resource/Shutterstock.com

© Stuart Miles/Shutterstock.com

5. Have a Clear Purpose and Format. Be sure to remind your audience members what your goal is immediately at the start of the session. Although you already included this in your initial meeting invitation, be sure to reiterate why you have called everyone together. In addition, what type of meeting are you hosting? A meeting to brainstorm for new procedures is very different than one where you are instructing employees about new initiatives. Define what type of interaction you expect from your audience. Tell them it is ok to engage and speak during the presentation or if you would prefer to hold all questions until the end so you are sure to cover the content.

6. Stick to Your Plan. You have a clear purpose of what information you need to review. Remember the agenda, goals, and point of conducting the meeting in the first place. You only have a set amount of time with all of the individuals together. Be sure to get through your plan of attack, and if you end a little early – fantastic!

7. Additional Meeting vs. Follow-up. Despite our best efforts, we cannot always foresee problems with our plan. It may not be until during the meeting that everyone realizes something will not work. Do not panic – it happens! (Just try to avoid it happening frequently!) This may mean you have to go back to the drawing board, do some additional research on processes, and then call another meeting. However, if everything goes smoothly, then a second meeting may not be necessary. As the organizer, it is your job to provide any follow-up documentation about the meeting to the audience members (collection of ideas discussed, steps moving forward, the consensus of the group, etc.). Be clear about how and when you will provide that information to your team.

Virtual Meetings

The pandemic shifted how many leaders host meetings. According to a Bureau of Labor Statistics report (2021) the percent of employees who worked from home doubled in the year 2020 compared to two years prior. However, even as the pandemic situation improved, many organizations realized significant benefits from continuing work from home models, virtual meetings, etc. Collins' (2021) stated, "We now see that workers can be just as productive in a hybrid environment compared to the perception that they wouldn't be in an office" (p. 02b).

When attending a virtual meeting, the same steps apply as previously discussed above for in-person meetings: avoid prejudgment, write down information, review/clarify before leaving, etc. However, the "setting a good example" step requires additional explanation when in a virtual environment.

A) In face-to-face meetings your colleagues and supervisors can visibly see if you are paying attention, chatting with others during the meeting, or playing on your phone. The temptation with a virtual meeting is to turn off your camera so your coworkers cannot see what you are doing. Plus, you can send private chat messages to co-workers while the meeting is happening. Even if you do not look your best, it shows respect to the presenter to turn your camera on so they can see their audience's faces! In addition, being visible can help force good listening practices and focus on what is discussed in the meeting. With your camera on, make every effort to concentrate on the speaker and not looking/typing on another screen, scrolling on your phone, etc.

B) Although you want to stay visible, keep your microphone turned off until you need to speak. The larger the group, the more distracting the background noise becomes for both the speaker and the audience.

C) Avoid filters and distracting backgrounds. Although filters are funny, they do not always portray a professional image. Selecting a background may be appropriate if you do not want your audience to focus on the items behind you like what books are on your shelves, people walking by, or a messy living room. Keep to professional and/or generic images as your background so that you remain the focus of the screenshot. Just like filters, although funny to be pictured in cartoon settings, next to celebrities, or sitting in the White House the line between humorous and unprofessional can become blurred.

After understanding the additional considerations of face-to-face versus virtual meetings as an audience member, we now need to understand the added factors in hosting a virtual session. Once again, some of the same rules apply as a face-to-face session including assessing if a meeting is necessary, who needs to be present, and having a clear agenda for the meeting. Unfortunately, it can be even more difficult to keep an audience's attention in a virtual environment so consider these elements when planning a session.

A) Choose the right technology. DeRosa (2011) noted to consider the purpose of your meeting and types of interaction necessary when selecting what virtual platform to use. Do you need to solicit feedback? Poll your audience? Record the session? Present simultaneously with a PowerPoint? Different conferencing tools will have pros and cons to consider when hosting your meeting. Also be sure to include any instructions about how to download the appropriate tool/program, check for any software updates, and conduct a test prior to the session.

B) Consider any time zone differences. Remember if you are meeting with members of different branch offices or customers from across the country/world, a 2 p.m. meeting in your time zone could be 4 a.m. for another person.

C) Keep the meeting focused/on track. Despite your preparation and organization, your audience members are exposed to even more distractions in a virtual environment. So what can you do as a presenter to try to keep your team attentive? DeRosa (2011) noted three different practices to implement when a meeting is headed off the rails: observation, diagnosis, and intervention. Pay close attention to the conversations and interactions occurring among the group. Review the topic being discussed and determine if it relevant to the discussion, needs to be addressed at a later time, or completely off topic. Based on observations and determining if the topic is not valid for this meeting you would need to intervene and direct your team back to the task at hand.

Complaints in the Workplace

If you have ambitions to be any type of boss or leader within your organization, then prepare yourself to deal with all of the good and the bad that comes with the territory. As a supervisor, working through the negative situations is not the most pleasant part of the job. However, ignoring issues only makes problems persist or grow in intensity. It is important to understand the different types of complaints you will receive and how to properly manage them.

Before we go in-depth, it is important to remember that no matter what type of organization you are in (school, business, nonprofit, etc.), each place has a chain of command for how to assess and handle complaints. For example, at your college, the first step of the complaint process may be to speak with a department chair and not to the dean (despite what popular culture displays). Review policies and handbooks to ensure the situation follows proper procedure.

© ESB Professional/Shutterstock.com

Legitimate Issues

The first type of complaint concerns true issues within the organization. They could include all types of situations from budgetary concerns, policy, or personnel matters. Remember, they are serious matters that deserve our attention. So, if one of your employees comes to talk to you about a work issue, here are some things to keep in mind.

1. Listen, Do not Speak. The person came to you for a reason so allow them to have the floor and be able to fully express themselves. Do not interrupt; do not ask questions (yet). Just let the person speak. Sometimes, this may solve the problem in itself. Maybe the person just needs to vent frustration and be heard by someone else. They may find the answer to the issue just talking through the details. Even if they still need the next steps, the key is you allowed them the opportunity to speak their mind and be heard.

2. Summarize the Issue(s). After the person finished expressing their concerns, repeat back the key points and summarize their thoughts. It is the opportunity for clarification of any misunderstandings, but it also validates that you were truly listening to what they had to say. This shows that you understand what they are trying to communicate.

3. Keep a Neutral Position. Even if you whole-heartedly believe in what the person is presenting, you cannot "show your cards" or reveal your personal beliefs on the issue. What if the person is expressing concern about another coworker? Remember you have only heard one side of the story, so it is unwise to make a decision without having all of the facts. Same with any policy or procedure concerns; usually we cannot just change a process without involving others in the decision.

4. Ask about Solutions. So, the individual came to you and expressed their concerns; now what do they want? If it is just a vent session, then your job is done. Yeah! Do not get your hopes up though; it is usually not that easy. Keep this in mind if you plan to speak with a supervisor about an issue to have some potential solutions in mind. What does the person see as a potential solution? They may already know the best ways to improve a process because it is part of their daily responsibilities.

5. Explain Your Role. As previously mentioned, we cannot always make changes immediately without gathering more information or involving other people in the organization. Let the person know

© Cressida studio/Shutterstock.com

that you will look into the matter and/or discuss the concern with the appropriate parties and will come back to them with an answer.

6. Close the Loop. Indicate how and when they can expect a response. For example, "Give me a week and I'll come talk to you during your office hours about what I find out." "I have a meeting with X this afternoon so I will follow up about your concern in an email after speaking with them." Even if the answer is not what the individual wanted, you have to follow through and show them you did listen to them, took their concerns seriously, and went through the process completely. Closing the loop also helps to build trust with your colleagues in hopes they feel comfortable to speak to you again when future situations arise.

© Michael R Ross/Shutterstock.com

Faux Issues

This type of complaints may first appear as though they are true issues, but once the person starts talking, they often derive from your whiners and complainers within an organization. Even with this type of situation, there are procedural steps you still have to follow to ensure you have crossed your t's and dotted the i's, if anything is questioned later.

1. Listen, Do not Speak. Initially, you have to let the person have the floor to discover why they are coming to speak with you. Even though 99 times out of 100, this person is coming to gripe about the same drama they always complain about, the one time you do not listen will be the one time they have

© txking/Shutterstock.com

a legitimate issue to address. Protect yourself and make sure you give them the same opportunity as anyone else to speak. Disregarding their concerns may cause you to be the one in trouble!

2. Recognize Feelings. After you have heard the "concern," you still want to acknowledge the person and their feelings on the issue. Blowing them off will not solve the problem and may only intensify the situation if they decide to go to the next step in the chain of command because you did not listen.

3. Create an Action Plan. After the person finishes speaking, create a plan of attack moving forward, noting specific tasks you want them to do or try on the job. There are several things that may come of the situation. 1) They may attempt the plans and solve the problem, 2) They attempt the plans, it does not work but shows the person's willingness to try alternatives, or 3) They do not attempt any corrective measures. Unfortunately, number three is often the result. Complainers do not want to fix the problem, otherwise what do they have to complain about?

© iQoncept/Shutterstock.com

4. Shut Down Future Attempts. When the person approaches you again about the same issues, you can refer back to the action plan created and ask how things are going, what steps have they tried, etc. The action plan is a good measure for you as a supervisor to show evidence that you met with the individual and made a combined effort to resolve their concerns. If the individual is unwilling to try any of the suggestions, then you have nothing further to add. At that point, the conversation can end because you laid out a plan that was not attempted, and you always have other issues pressing as a leader!

Improve Your Listening Skills

Despite all of the meetings and conversations we sit through, we usually do not enter into those situations planning to be a bad listener. However, there are steps we can take to keep our listening behaviors in check.

© gguy/Shutterstock.com

Focus Your Efforts

We discussed how the 'Attend' step in listening is probably the most difficult. Keep this in mind, as you enter your communication interaction, and try to make a conscious effort to give the speaker your undivided attention. Turn off distractions if you can (let others know if you are going into a meeting, put your phone on vibrate/silent) to prevent additional temptations to not focus. In addition, try to put yourself in the speaker's shoes. Remember the nerves and anxiety you feel when you have to present? Give that person the respect you would hope to receive if you were giving the speech. In addition, try to see the problem/issue from the presenter's perspective. They are communicating about this topic for a reason, so try to figure out why it is so important to them.

Pay Attention

Yes, you have the actual words to listen to, but also look at the nonverbal cues of the person speaking. What can you tell based on their body language, eye contact, or their tone of voice? By paying close attention to their entire message, you can avoid literal listening and really understand what they are trying to communicate.

Know Your Listening Role

What is your goal in the communication interaction? Is the person coming to you to just vent? Are they looking for a solution? Maybe it is a larger problem that requires more of your time and energy. No matter which scenario you face, you still have to listen carefully to the person speaking. Through giving them your undivided attention and paying close attention to their words and emotions expressed during the conversation, you can often decipher what they need from you after they have finished speaking. If you cannot figure it out, ask them!

This chapter examined listening concepts, the application of good listening techniques, and the dos and don'ts of running or participating in meetings in the workplace. There is no doubt about it, listening is an extremely difficult task (especially for an extended period of time). However, by understanding the listening process and the different obstacles that can get in our way, you can make positive strides toward becoming a better listener in your everyday life and in the workplace. Recognizing our weaknesses and choosing to try and become engaged and active while in conversations is an important first step in becoming a good listener.

REFERENCES

Collins, T. (2021, November 12). Survey: Many Us workers hope to stay remote after pandemic. *USA Today, 0734-7456*, 01b–02b.

DeRosa, D. (2011, August). Hello, is anybody out there? Six Steps to High Impact V-Meetings. *T+D, 65*(8), 28–29.

Johromi, V. K., Tabatabaee, S. S., Abdar, Z. E., & Rajabi, M. (2016). Active listening: The key of successful communication in hospital managers. *Electronic Physician, 8*(3), 2123-2128.

Watson, K., Barker, L., & Weaver, J. (1995). The listening styles profile (LSP-16): Development and validation of an instrument to assess four listening styles. *International Journal of Listening, 9*, 1-13.

Watson, L. (2015). Humans have shorter attention span than goldfish, thanks to smartphones. *The Telegraph*. Retrieved from: http://www.telegraph.co.uk/science/2016/03/12/humans-have-shorter-attention-span-than-goldfish-thanks-to-smart/.

15 The Art of Good Speaking in Business and Beyond: Delivery

Speaking and communicating in public, regardless of the context or organization, puts everyone in the role of "critic." The speaker criticizes their own performance, audience members leave thinking a speaker was inspiring or awful, and sometimes we do or do not accomplish our goal(s) as a presenter. This chapter discusses what many students seek in our classes: how to improve. All of the things discussed to this point only help so much unless a student learns how to continuously improve beyond this class and college. There are many ways to practice and rehearse your presentation, and almost none of them require a mirror. This chapter will cover the art of rehearsal and delivery, and how to make your presentation the most charismatic and dynamic it can be.

Delivery Styles

We discussed structure and content, citations and research, but it is also time to discuss how to deliver your presentation. There are four major ways to deliver your presentation, each with its own pros, cons, and purpose. Some of these delivery methods you already know and call by more informal names like, "on-the-fly" or "winging it." Let's explore these options now.

Impromptu

Impromptu speaking may be the most common form of business and professional presentations. **Impromptu** translates to "speaking without preparation or notes." However, "winging-it" and "on-the-fly" have more radical connotations like, "let's hope this doesn't suck" or "I'll just hope for the best." True Impromptu speaking is a bit more formal than this. Think about an interview situation. You do not always know what will be asked of you in a job interview; however, you often have a good idea of some of the questions that

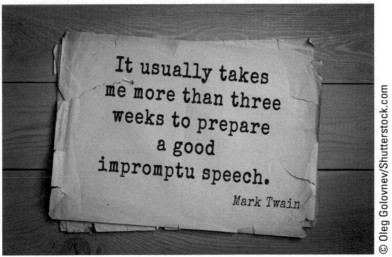

It usually takes me more than three weeks to prepare a good impromptu speech.

Mark Twain

© Oleg Golovnev/Shutterstock.com

will be raised about your goals, previous experience, work ethic and so on. Even if asked a question you did not anticipate, you are expected to come up with a poignant, knowledgeable response in a matter of seconds to impress and (hopefully) land a job. It takes practice to pull off a good impromptu presentation.

1. Thinking. When asked to speak on the spot, or without preparation, take a moment to think about your thesis. How will you answer this question? What are the two to four main points you want to convey? Remember, there is a reason you have been asked to speak on this subject; the person asking should allow you a moment to pull together a few thoughts.
2. Use structure! Just because you are thinking and speaking on the spot does not mean you should relinquish all the things you know about structure. If someone asks you a detailed question, provide them structure like this: "Sure, we can discuss XYZ and I feel there will be TWO main things to focus on in marketing. First. . . ., Second. . . .; so those are the main concerns for our team when it comes to marketing." Using this structure will save your nerves and fears and provide an easy roadmap for your audience to follow.
3. Rehearse. Yes—rehearse on-the-spot speaking. Recall earlier we mentioned it takes 10,000 hours to create a habit. Some of the best speakers you can think of in your office, organization, friend group, or class have been speaking for some time. To be good at impromptu speaking, it takes practice. We suggest picking topics and working through the structure in 30 second to 1 minute practice runs in your car, office, or the gym. Actually form thesis statements and run through short mini-speeches.

Manuscripted

The type of speech or presentation many of us were brought up delivering is the **manuscripted** speech. This is the delivery style where the presenter has written the entire presentation word-for-word on a script paper and is presenting from that script. Many speakers are familiar with this style because this is how many presenters have been speaking since they were young. Middle school speeches and wedding addresses have been given in this format for years by speakers with little or no training.

As with many things, there are pros and cons to using this style of presentation. On one hand, everything you will say is prepared in front of you, so the idea of "losing your train of thought" does not really unnerve people. However, this also brings with it a greater responsibility to rehearse. Many speakers find when they approach the front of the room, table, or stage that their nerves get the better of them. Then, in an effort to make no mistakes, they begin to read (really read) their speech word-for-word sounding like a student reading aloud in class to a room of sleepy fellow students. Thus, the energy, eye contact, and charisma are lacking. Immediacy is gone.

© Syda Productions/Shutterstock.com

Scripted speeches when written well (have we mentioned structure?) are important because they lessen the chance a speaker will forget a very important point. Scripted speeches also allow for more novice speakers to speak for a pre-determined amount of time. Once a speaker begins rehearsing their scripted speech over-and-over, it typically runs around the same amount of time each time. So, if you have been asked to speak for 3 minutes—then a scripted 3-minute speech may be the way to go, so you do not run over or under program time. However, in the business context, often people are not speaking from scripted remarks; they are in interviews, interviewing, reporting, and participating in a last minute briefing—all forms of speaking and communicating.

"Remember, I'm behind you all the way. WAY behind you."

Consider the persuasion and hostile audience situations discussed. If you have to deliver bad news (ex. layoffs) to employees, you definitely want to ensure you have all the facts and information to present exactly as it was handed down to you. This is new to some recent graduates who made many speeches, using other styles, during their college career. So, we hope you pay attention to the context that dictates what style to implement.

Memorized

As the title indicates, this delivery style is presenting your speech – memorized. It is different from impromptu because with **memorized** you completely script or fully outline your presentation, and then spend time learning it word-for-word or major concept for major concept. The memorized delivery has many of the same pros as the manuscripted delivery, but it takes the effort to the next level for more eye contact and engagement. Memorizing a speech, script, or outline is a lot of work. In many cases, the results pay off, but you do run the risk of looking over-rehearsed, automated, or robotic.

You have heard memorized speeches at museums, aquariums, maybe even some car dealerships—it's generally pretty easy to know when someone launches into a "script" even if they are not holding one. We posit in your professional career you will probably use a fully memorized presentation style very rarely. Remember—this is different than "knowing your stuff" and presenting an impromptu speech. This is fully memorizing a script.

Extemporaneous

Big word–big results. **Extemporaneous** means "speaking from notes." This is the delivery format that is happily between impromptu and scripted. The presenter creates a speaking outline or notes of main points, and then presents from those notes. You do not write down word-for-word what you will say (this turns into manuscripted quite quickly). Instead, you prepare what is called a speaking outline and rehearse using those notes. The key is to increase the eye contact as best you can while relying on the notes to not forget any key information. This delivery works very well in business and professional contexts because facts, figures, and quotes are best presented from notes—so they are accurate. Your audience in this scenario is very forgiving because they appreciate your accuracy to detail in relaying correct and accurate information from those notes.

Delivery Styles and Advantages

STYLE	PROS	CONS
Impromptu	• Appears natural and conversational • Works well in interviews • No notes allows for maximum eye-contact • Can be used with effective movement	• Actually needs practice at home/ahead of time • Newer speakers can get lost in their thoughts • May be too short or too long for allotted speaking time
Manuscript	• Speaker has document containing entire speech • Can be rehearsed and timed for exact length of speaking engagement • Speaker will not ramble or mis-speak in the moment	• Sounds robotic, and unnatural • Disallows for maximum eye-contact • If not practiced, speaker will read to audience
Memorized	• Maximum eye-contact • Can be timed for exact speaking time allotment • Can be used with effective movement	• Potential for speaker to sound "canned" or fake • If speaker loses train of thought, it may be hard to recover
Extemporaneous	• Allows for greater eye-contact than manuscripted • Sounds natural/professional • Looks professional/referral to notes for names and references	• Needs rehearsal so speaker does not read notes • Still has notes/paper/ipad

Depending on the venue for your presentation, it might be time to rethink the 3×5 note cards. Other options might include using a typed half sheet of printer paper, a folded piece of printed/printer paper, your tablet or phone, or even your small computer. Whichever your choice, make sure to practice using it ahead of time. If you shake when you get nervous, then maybe sheets of paper are not the best choice as the paper will shake along with you. Speakers fumbling with iPads look just as awkward as a presenter holding a note card that resembles a recipe. Just consider the overall perception of the event. Smartphones have long celebrated their 15 year anniversary, yet, to date we have rarely seen someone make a beautifully presented speech while using a phone for notes. Often the phones home screens close on the speaker, or the font is too small to read. Many of these issues can be avoided by rehearsing. However, we ask you to consider if using your phone for notes matches the rest of the context. Are you in a super-formal or highly elegant situation? Might the phone look to technical? Too casual? Or, are you presenting technological information in a progressive setting? Then perhaps with some practice the phone is right for this scenario. As with everything, remember to outline, use structure, and practice!

Delivery

It's time to discuss the actual art and science of delivering your presentations with charisma, style, grace, and professionalism. To this point, you have your content, your organizational pattern, checked your sources, and created your outline. You have chosen your delivery method and now it is time to refine how you make the presentation unique compared to other speakers. For the following discussion, we are going to assume the context of a professional presentation, one given either in class or in a conference style room where you will be standing up front and possibly be using a projection screen. We recognized and have discussed different types of presentations: interviews, panel discussions, reports, roundtables, etc. For the next few minutes, we are thinking stand-and-deliver; all eyes on you—pitch or presentation.

The Podium

Let's start with the classics. The podium, the lectern. Many of us grew up using a podium for the few times we made a public presentation. Music rooms, middle schools, churches, and baseball banquets across the country house podiums where speakers will rest their notes or names of those they are recognizing. There is nothing wrong with podiums. They offer classic style, grace, and elegance. The problems lie with the training (or lack thereof) of how to use a podium within the context of a professional style presentation in the business or organizational world.

Unless you are speaking on a stage with a smart podium geared for computer control and electronics, we guess you will not find too many podiums in professional situations across the country—and that's the point here. We ask students to make professional and polished presentations, but we put them in contexts more attuned to baseball banquets and presidential speeches. However, no one pitching a product or service should be hiding behind a podium.

The speaker should be out close to the audience to make a connection and be perceived as likable. Think about it! If you have ever watched a TedTalk, you will rarely see the speaker hiding behind a podium. Ted's motto, "Ideas worth spreading," manifests itself in the delivery style of the speakers. So, it's time to ditch that podium and move closer to your screen, closer to your audience, closer to success!

Now What?

OK, so you are out from behind the podium, now what? First, arrange the room the way you want it. It is okay to politely ask people to move if you need to use their table for your notes. That's right—it is professional to set your notes on the front table or the boardroom table, especially with longer or group presentations. Additionally, do not set these notes in front of your projection screen. Many speakers walk in front of the LED projector. Make sure you are cognizant of where you are standing.

Get yourself a "clicker." Having something to advance slides while you walk around will give you a freedom you have never experienced. It's exciting (and yes, it can be scary the first time!). Once you are away from that podium, you will never want to go back. Clickers look professional and are easy to operate.

Plan your movement. This one is new for almost all speakers who have not been formally trained. Many speakers are told to "move around" but what does that even mean? It does not (or should not) mean pace around. Sometimes, pacing around like a tennis ball is actually worse than standing behind a podium. Instead, you must plan your movement. Not a carefully choreographed Dancing with the Stars piece, but you should map out on your paper where you will be when you are making certain points within your presentation. In the speaking world, this is called walking with purpose or moving with purpose. Consider mapping out your entire talk like a football play.

Think of it: your introduction begins nearer the screen and you complete your hook and components there. Upon your transition, you move up and slightly right to make your first point. While standing there, you talk TO your audience and occasionally refer left to the screen. To make your second point, you transition and walk across the screen's field to the other side of it. There you make your second point while talking TO your audience and occasionally referring to the slide. You take a step or two for transition to your third point (we suggest a step closer to the screen). There, you finish your presentation body. You walk and talk for a transition over to where you began to end memorably and conclude. BAM! A lot to handle? We created this figure for you already! Refer back to where we discussed transitions and the Triangle Method.

The movement piece feels awkward to new speakers, but it looks so much more dynamic to the audience. Of course, you need to rehearse. If you find yourself in odd-shaped rooms or situations, then you must adjust accordingly. If scripted movement is overwhelming, then start with smaller adjustments through your presentation. Try to avoid planting your feet in one place for the entire presentation (and do not lock your knees!). Movement helps the audience stay focused and the speaker physically organize his or her presentations.

Of final mention here, masks. The Covid pandemic brought with it physical distancing and the wearing of masks. Unfortunately, these practices negate years of effective speech delivery research. We know that closeness and perceived closeness between speaker and audience increases likability. We know that almost all non-verbal communication comes from the face. Covid altered these behaviors. To note, if you encounter someone saying, "class is just better in person," or, "yoga class is difficult online," but they cannot articulate why. This is why. The non-verbal communication cues were altered by computers, distancing, and masks, making it more difficult to receive messages. In all cases, if you have to speak with a mask or from a distance, work on increasing your presence by incorporating other techniques during delivery. This may include asking the audience members to stand-up and/or repeat things you ask. You might consider a paper handout or a parting piece of collateral to be more memorable. There are many ways to increase "high-touch" practices without actually being close to your front row. We just ask if you are required to use a mask in the future (maybe a retirement community or hospital), consider ways to increase non-verbal presence to make up for the lost facial expressions.

What Not to Do!

Teaching about delivery can sometimes seem a little negative because often it is easier to tell people what NOT to do rather than what TO do. This comes from undoing many years of self-learned bad habits. Here, we collegially highlight some things to stay away from when making a professional pitch or presentation.

1. Do not turn your back on your audience. Audiences do not want to be read to. If you don't know your material well enough maybe you should not present it quite yet.

2. Do not go in without practicing (physically get up and walk around your office or hotel room). Trust us. It helps calm the nerves in those final moments before entering to give a presentation.

3. Do NOT tell the audience how a) nervous, b) unprepared, c) out of sorts you are. Audiences can be merciless—do not

give them something else to dislike about you. Audiences can be supportive because most of them would rather you be up there than them. So, at least act the professional part. The audience does not know unless you tell them! The "fake it, 'til you make it" concept applies here.

4. Do NOT tell the audience how much you don't do, like, or understand the technology of your speech e.g., type of computer, screen, clicker, etc. Remember you CHOSE this modality to make your presentation. Why would not you know how it works. The solution: practice!

5. Do not start by introducing your topic and then launching into a "speech." Instead work your topic/name into your presentation, so you look excellent!

6. Do not spout negative self-talk. When you are in the audience, at lunch, or in the board room, people will remember what you say to them. If you tell a colleague at lunch you are nervous or unprepared for your upcoming presentation, that will stick in their mind when you get up to present. Remember ears are everywhere and you never know whose they are.

7. Do not make unprofessional PowerPoints. Seriously No, trust us. It's not cute, energizing, or novel to simply throw words on a screen and expect an audience to *want* that. Audiences have come to lament PowerPoints so much that even if the information is important, they will tune out. Just. Be. Careful.

8. Do not apologize. Never tell an audience you are sorry for any of your own work. "Sorry this is boring, sorry this is dull, sorry . . . sorry . . . sorry." Stop. Instead, fix the problem ahead of time in order to create a more positive atmosphere. Instead of being sorry, be prepared.

9. Do not mispronounce people's names, especially those foreign in American English. This does two things. 1) It shows you have never said the word aloud before which means you didn't rehearse and 2) It can be degrading to that person's name. Americans often have a weird (bad?) habit of butchering foreign names and thinking it's normal. Just practice the name ahead of time. And remember, if you are citing a source and that person is not in the audience, no one will know better if you said it wrong or not. Remember that!

10. Do not worry about your nerves. Some nerves are good (and normal). If you rehearsed and did what you were supposed to, you should have fun and be fine!

Some things you should consider doing when making your professional presentation.

1. Thank the person who invited you. In a classroom speech you could say, "Many thanks to Dr. Smith for including this opportunity in her assignments. With that, I have a question for everyone!" And roll into your attention-getter. This gets you in the habit of practicing for your professional contexts.

2. Do smile! (But not forced "creepy" smile.) Just relax and try to be as much like yourself as possible.

3. Do talk directly to the audience. Feel free to ask them questions and have a "discussion". Of course, your material and the setting will better dictate this, but it is OK. Some speakers have been trained (incorrectly) not to break the fourth wall.

4. Do tell an audience that you are happy to be with them.

5. Do tell an audience why you chose this topic, or why you were invited to speak. An audience wants to know why you care—tell them.

6. Do practice.

7. Do practice some more.

8. Do test your technology ahead of time if that opportunity is available to you. Run slides, sounds, and links ahead of time. Remember to carry all files over along with PowerPoint and Keynote (and ALWAYS have a backup plan).

9. Do own your topic, your information, and your expertise. Remember—no apologies.

10. Do acknowledge when you mis-spoke as to get your facts right. Do not apologize for correct information, though.
11. Have fun!

Speaking can be nerve-wracking for many people. We hope our discussion in this chapter will help ease nerves as they relate to process and delivery. We offered four types of delivery methods (process) and discussed some elements of physicality when presenting a professional pitch or speech. Of course, it is difficult for a delivery chapter to be all things to all speakers. Bottom line: prepare and practice! The more [correct] speaking opportunities one gets, the better, more confident, and professional that speaker will become.

If you are a student in the middle of your college experience, one way to improve speaking skills is to volunteer to present and speak as much as possible. Tell your instructors you are working on this skill. Many people will be happy to hear this and help to incorporate you into their agendas. The same thing goes at work. Offer to lead meetings and try new things. The more new situations you try, the more familiar they will be to you when they arise at work or school. Good luck!

16 The Art of Good Writing and Technology

In professional settings it is important you consider your writing, communication style, and etiquette. All communication in the workplace should be purposeful, include relevant information, be clear, and effective. As a professional, you will write all sorts of documents from emails to proposals. The following chapter identifies what to consider when formatting a formal written document, how to send email, and how to engage in casual communication through texting. This chapter also discusses how to appropriately engage with technology in the workplace through electronic security and netiquette.

Written Documents

When working with written documents it is important to think about *layout* and *typography* to ensure your document is visually appealing and easy to read. The following guidelines will help you maintain professional credibility while you are communicating through written documents. These guidelines presented reflect standard formatting practices; however, your industry or field might have different expectations. When first hired, take time to observe the written practices within your organization to ensure you are complying with their standards.

Page Layout

- Indentation: It is standard practice for first line of a new paragraph to be indented .5 inches. You can do this by pressing the tab key once.
- Justification: Justified text means there is a clear vertical line down one and/or both margins. Standard documents are left-justified, but you can select the option of full-justified to have both sides lined up (but it will impact your spacing!).
- Line Spacing: When sending a letter maintain a single-spaced line between sentences with line breaks between paragraphs. In contrast, papers submitted for your class are often double-spaced to allow room for the instructor to provide feedback and/or comments.
- Margins: When opening a new Word document your margins will most likely be set at "normal," which is a 1-inch margin all around. However, you can adjust or customize this by going to the Layout tab and selecting the Margins drop-down menu.
- White Space: White space are areas within the document that do not include text, images, or graphs. For example, margins are considered white space. Strategically use white space to emphasize the content within the document. Remember building your resume? You wanted to limit the white space to maximize your page.

Typography

The two main categories of typeface are serif and sans serif. A serif typeface includes small extenders on the letters where sans serif has a more standardized look. Both are acceptable, but there are multiple options to select within both categories.

Professional Font Options:

- Arial and Helvetica are the most common sans serif options due to its clean and legible look. American Airlines, American Apparel, and The North Face use a similar logo font.
- Times New Roman and Garamond are popular serif typefaces with a natural creative look. Apple and Microsoft Windows use a font style similar to Garamond as a text in their products.
- Futura has a strong stylish look that can provide a touch of creativity to your document. Nike, Supreme, and Red Bull use a logo font that is similar to Futura.
- Sabon has a soft curvy look. Vogue and Esquire use a font that is similar to Sabon in their headlines.

- Font size: It is standard practice that documents are written in 12-point font.
- Boldface and Underlining: Use to strategically emphasize a word or phrase. Use bold and underlining tools sparingly within your document. You want to be sure you draw attention to the important points and not overuse to the point the reader has no clue because 'everything' is marked as important!

Style and Tone

It all goes back to the beginning—audience analysis. Who is receiving your message? As discussed in the first chapter, consider who your audience is, their expectations, and their preferred communication approach. Specifically we are talking about the style and tone of a written document. Writing style (such as language choices), sentence structure, and paragraph formatting are contingent on the context the written document is being produced. However, writing in an active voice is considered the standard writing style. To write in an **active voice** place the subject of the sentence before the verb. Another tip is to avoid placing is, was, and were in front of the verb. (Sometimes it is best to write your thoughts down first and then edit the sentence.)

Passive: The contract is being signed by the client today.
Active: The client is signing the contract today.

Passive: The email was sent from my boss.
Active: My boss sent me an email.

Passive: Your memo was read by the entire office.
Active: The entire office read your memo.

Passive Words to Try to Avoid

Be	Was	Have	Do	Shall	May	Can
Am	Were	Has	Does	Will	Might	Could
Is	Being	Had	Did	Should	Must	
Are	Been			Would		

The purpose of the document determines the layout selected, font choice, and writing style. Above are some examples of standard practice. However, in a work context, documents should always be professional and sincere.

How to Email

© SpicyTruffel/Shutterstock.com

Emails are now one of the predominant forms of communication in a professional work environment. Technology allows us to send messages across the planet with a few clicks of a button. Due to the fact that communication can happen so quickly, there are often errors or mistakes. Below, you will learn how to structure and write an email as well as some pointers to avoid becoming the email pariah of the office.

Professors everywhere bemoan student emails written like text messages. In fact, if we had a dollar for every time a student emailed, "K. Tx," we could quit our jobs. Email messages are electronic communications that take the place of letters. Emails are more formal than text messages. They even follow the format of old school written letters. This section will teach you how to properly format an email and give you some practical reminders so you can put your best foot forward.

A traditional business letter format includes the following parts: header, address, greeting or salutation, body, and a closing signature. The same applies to your emails! The header of your email is also the subject line. Your subject should be a short and concise statement of the content of the email. Do not write out a long sentence or use capitalized words. Capitalized words in emails read as though the sender is yelling at the recipient. The address is clearly the person's email address that you are using. The greeting or salutation goes at the top of the body of the email and should be professional. "Hey Toby," is not an appropriate email greeting. Stick with the classics such as, "Good Morning Toby" or even an old fashioned "Dear Toby."

Keep the body of your email clear and direct. Please do not write a novel. Do not send an email as long as this textbook chapter! Instead, keep your email short and include pertinent information in an attachment. Even though electronic communication is a substitute for written documents, no one has the attention span to read a long email communication. Regarding your signature block and sign off, choose the contents carefully. Generally, you conclude your emails with a, "Thank you" or "Sincerely." Emails that include all kinds of random information in the signature block can be confusing, especially if unrelated. Your signature block also contains your contact information in case more follow up is needed. You do not need to have your picture or other random information. Links to your website or LinkedIn are appropriate in business.

Sample Email Template

To: Allen@email.com
From: Professor@email.com

Subject: Your Zoom Attire

Dear Allen,

Thank you for participating in our Zoom class discussion. Please note, students should be fully attired when attending class. Please wear a shirt to our next online class session. Let me know if you have any questions.

Thank you,

Professor ABC

Assistant Professor
College of Business
123 Main Street
Random Town, FL
(888) 888-8888

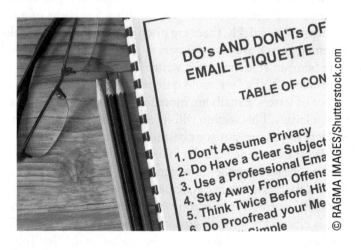

When it comes to the do's and don'ts of emails, follow some of the best practices:

- As a leader, set expectations of how/when you reply to messages. Yes, it is important to be responsive, but that does not always mean you have to reply within five minutes of receiving an email! Even if you have a 24-hour turnaround policy, some questions require research or input from other individuals before you can answer. If you need more time, notify the sender you received their message but require additional time to find an answer and will get back to them by a specific deadline with an update.

- Evaluate if you should send the email in the first place! Some messages are better in person or over the telephone. If the subject matter is lengthy or complicated, then perhaps it is better to schedule an in person meeting to discuss.
- Don't assume the recipient will reply or even see it. Some people are inundated with messages and it is easy to accidentally overlook them. Again, more formal or important messages may want to be delivered in a different format.
- Be mindful of the time of day that you send your emails. You may be a night owl, but it may appear unprofessional to send an email to your boss at 3 a.m. On the flip side, if you are the manager, you do not want to set a false expectation that you expect a reply from someone at 3 a.m. Best practice may be to save your emails as a draft and wait until business hours to send.
- Watch who you send the email to, especially the dreaded "Reply All!" Electronic communication happens faster than written communication so take time to make sure you are emailing the correct party. You do not want to accidentally send confidential client information to the wrong person. Also, only hit 'reply all' when absolutely necessary. As someone that receives a lot of email, it can be a frustrating waste of time to receive an email that does not pertain to the job.
- Only copy the people you want included in your email. Avoid **spamming**, or sending unsolicited emails to a large number of email addresses.
- Do not use emojis or smiley faces in professional or business emails. Remember, emailing is more formal than texting!
- Keep your tone respectful and polite. Get to the point of your message quickly and be concise.
- Spell check exists even for emails! There is no excuse for sending an email with a typo in it.
- When at work, do not email slang or joke memes. Emails can easily be forwarded to other people, and you do not want to get into trouble for misuse of company email. The same rule of thumb applies to talking trash about a coworker. Do not write anything negative or gossipy in an email as all it takes is one click for that email to be sent to that person. Think about how an outsider would review your message. For example, in a case of termination, and depending on your state, the fired employee may submit an Open Records Request which requires you to submit copies of all communication (emails, texts, etc.) pertaining to that individual. Remember— nothing is private!
- If your email contains a request, be sure to thank the person for their consideration.
- Words in all caps mean you are SHOUTING! Avoid using in formal work emails.

I'm so happy...

© DanIce/Shutterstock.com

What is wrong with this email? See how many errors you can find:

> To: Professor@email.com
> From: Allen@email.com
> CC: Entireclass@email.com
>
> Subject: Ur msg about my Clothing......MY BAD!
>
> Hey Proffessor,
>
> My bad about the shirt. I was in a hurry bc I just jumped out of the shower. I wont do that again bro! My bad! Dont fail me plz.
>
> Allen

© Rawpixel.com/Shutterstock.com

Considerations Before Sending

There are several factors to consider before deciding to send an email. One, consider the length of your email. The person you are communicating with is most likely also a busy professional. If your email is multi-paragraphs long it might be more efficient to simply call them. However, it would be appropriate to send a long email that included detailed instructions to reference at a later date. Two, is the topic time-sensitive or require an immediate response? If yes, then email is not the right medium. Do not expect your colleagues to be waiting on their computer for an email to arrive every minute of the day. Pick up the phone or go talk to the individual in person if it is an urgent matter. Three, sometimes we need to hear the person speaking to understand the tone of the message. As previously discussed, we communicate meaning through more than just the words said. So, before sending your email, ask yourself (1) can the message be simplified, (2) would the message be more clear communicated in person or a phone call, and (3) is the message confusing? Lastly, double check that you are sending the email to the correct person, the subject line summarizes what your email is about, and all documents are attached.

Electronic Security

In today's world, you can never be too safe when it comes to protecting yourself electronically. For example, some corporations do not even allow attachments to be received as they may contain viruses that wreak havoc on your computer and possibly the entire organization. Think before you open attachments and even some emails that you receive. **Phishing** scams often target work email accounts. These are scam emails that try to copy the look of a real email. Avoid opening emails that look suspicious or that are from people you do not know. Same goes with links contained in emails. Do not click on links sent by people you do not know or links that look odd. Multiple organizations suffered attacks from ransomware and lost access to all of their information unless a ransom is paid.

It is in your best interest to check with your company's information technology department about virus software and ways to protect yourself. They can help you update your technology with protection software and may have rules about passwords. Also be aware of who has access to your computer when you walk away from your desk. Do not leave important documents visible on your screen if you need to go to the restroom, etc. Back up your data in case of a virus or a crash. Most importantly, do not give out personal information. You should not use your company's computer or phone for personal matters, but make sure you are also mindful of your own privacy.

Texting and Messaging Apps

If you need to send a message quickly the convenience of texting might be an appropriate medium. For example, if your organization or employers needs to send a mass alert they will most likely text to communicate across multiple departments. However, just like email, there are certain expectations to follow. When sending media, such as a link or picture, be sure to include an explanation *before* you send the media. An explanation provides context for the message. Complex or important topics need to be addressed formally versus in a text message. You can cause panic and frustration among your team by sending a one-line text message about

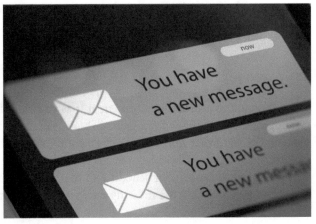

© ninefotostudio/Shutterstock.com

changing a policy with no explanation! Just like email, consider the time you are sending the text message (and be aware of different time zones). Stick to business hours unless it is an emergency (ex. if you are running late to work). When starting a new professional relationship with a coworker or client, you want to ease into casual communication such as texting until you know the other person is comfortable with informality. Lastly, if you dictate your message verbally be sure to double-check for any errors.

Zooming

Zoom and virtual meetings are more and more commonplace thanks to the pandemic. In addition to wearing proper clothing on a Zoom, there are a number of best practices that exist for virtual meetings (also discussed in the Listening and Meetings chapter).

Background

Be considerate of your background for a virtual meeting. If you are attending class from your dorm room, perhaps pick up your dirty laundry in the back. The same applies for work meetings. You want to find a desk or table with a clean background. You also want to have good lighting so that the people in the meeting can clearly see you. If you are sitting in front of a window you may be backlit and it will be hard for people to see your face.

Posture and Eye Contact

Do NOT lay in bed for your virtual appointments. Working or attending class from home does not give you a free pass to lounge around. Find a chair that will give you a confident posture that also positions your camera at the same level as your face so you are not looking down. Speaking of eye contact, if you are on the computer avoid looking down at your cell phone or texting. It is very obvious when someone is playing on their phone instead of engaging with others in a meeting. Their eyes shift downward and their shoulders slump forward.

Cameras

Be sure to have your cameras on folks! It is appropriate to turn off your cameras if you are running to the restroom, need to answer a phone call, etc. We have seen examples on social media (and even used in commercials) where a badly angled camera reveals moments in the bathroom, wearing only boxer shorts, etc. That said, place your cameras facing you so that you can make good eye contact, but turn them off for breaks (and mute as well!).

Behavior

While you are in a virtual meeting, treat it as you would a normal in-person meeting. It is not the time to go digging in your closet for a pair of shoes, to take a drive, cook dinner, be in the bathroom of a night-club, or do any other non-meeting behavior. (We wish these were made up examples instead of actual experiences!) There is nothing wrong with drinking a cup of coffee, but certainly do not fill your cup with margaritas. Block your schedule so that you are able to focus on the meeting and not other errands or other actions during the meeting that would distract yourself or others.

Meeting Rules Apply

It is appropriate to make a little bit of small talk at the start of a virtual meeting. However, whoever is leading the meeting will likely take charge and get things rolling when appropriate. As such, the same rules apply. Be respectful of others' ideas and opinions. Try not to speak over each other. This is particularly true in a virtual format. It can be hard to know when someone is done speaking and it is your turn. Use the features like chats or raising the cartoon hands rather than simply interrupting someone.

© Rido/Shutterstock.com

Netiquette

Netiquette describes how to communicate properly either electronically or in a virtual space. Some of the netiquette rules you can gleam from above in the previous sections about emails and virtual meetings. While you should be properly engaged in a meeting online, you should also be mindful of other people's time. Avoid wasting time during meetings by coming unprepared or oblivious about how to operate the technology. Also, avoid delaying responding to emails when you can. Emails are faster than written letters and may demand a faster reply. While it is possible to accidentally miss an email or need to time for further research, it is considered rude to intentionally not reply.

Use respectful language when communicating online. Avoid **flaming**, or criticizing individuals in an email or discussion forum using inappropriate language. It is expected to debate and discuss topics, but do not make your comments personal attacks on someone or their ideas. Think about the space where you are communicating. Text messages may be more casual and emojis may even be appropriate. However, emails are slightly more formal and therefore require a bit more consideration before you hit send. Even though you may not be physically face to face with someone, it does not mean you can be informal or even rude. Electronic communication is easily recorded and you do not want to be that person accused of harassment just because you sent a joke that is misconstrued. Be respectful of work rules and do not send jokes as they really are not appropriate for the workplace.

Lastly, make yourself look good! Spell check all messages regardless of the format. Update your social media profiles and LinkedIn account. Be polite and respectful with your tone and content. Think before you hit send and ask yourself how you would feel to receive that type of message.

Conclusion

As technology advances you will have more communication options to choose from than ever before! While this makes our lives easier in many respects, it can also cause some complications in the work environment. Be mindful that you are choosing the best format to communicate based on your audience and the type of message. Respect others' privacy and protect yourself and information from hackers. Leave the personal stuff, complaints, and inappropriate jokes at home. Spend time reviewing everything that you write, whether it be a typed letter or an electronic communication. As our options to communicate faster increase, it is a good idea to also slow down and think before you hit send!

References

Guynn, J. (2022, March 4). *'Ticking time bomb': Russian ransomware attacks are coming. What small business should do right now.* USA Today. Retrieved March 7, 2022, from https://www.usatoday.com/story/money/business/smallbusiness/2022/03/04/small-business-ukraine-russia-ransomware-attack/9379667002/

17 Group Communication

Call them committees, task forces, groups, teams, you name it—group communication is an integral part of the workplace. Your initial reaction may be to growl whenever you hear the words "group project" in your classes, but trust us, those assignments serve as good practice models for those group tasks you will have to complete on the job. In this chapter, we will discuss group characteristics, pros and cons of group work, and the problem-solving process.

So what constitutes a group? A basic definition is having three or more people who come together/ depend on one another to achieve a common goal. Often groups are formed for a specific purpose (goal) and then disband once the task is complete. Think about study groups, projects for class, committee work, etc. Each team has a specific end goal to achieve, and there is no need to continue interaction once the task is complete. However, this does not mean the relationship ends. Oftentimes, we develop new friends and add to our network of acquaintances that we can turn to in the future.

Group Characteristics

Jensen and Chilberg (1991) introduced six characteristics that make up a group: common goals, network, interdependence, structured relations, norms, and a sense of wholeness. The first is having the common goal.

The obvious goal is the task assigned to the group; however, at what level (and what effort) also goes into establishing the goal. Finishing a group project is one thing; trying to earn an A on an assignment is a different goal! Next is the network of communication that exists. Each person communicates differently and has different expectations. (Remember our discussions about culture and generations in the workplace?) Not only can the message differ, but also the channel used to deliver the message. Are you meeting face-to-face? Working online? Using text messages? It all creates a network among the group members.

Next is behavioral interdependence, which can be either task or relational. Task refers to the different jobs each group member completes individually, but also impacts each group member and the project as a whole; relational interdependence looks at the emotions between group members and how they influence one another. Think of dropping a stone in pool of water; the immediate impact is what the individual completes, but the ripples represent how it affects others around them. Structured relations go along with

the interactions experienced by group members, as they deal with the different roles each group member takes on throughout the process. We will discuss group roles in-depth later in this chapter.

The final two characteristics are shared norms and the perception of wholeness. "Norms are expectations for the group as a whole" (Jensen and Chilberg, 1991, p. 14).

What are the written/unwritten rules for how the group will function? Are there certain forms of communication that are mandated and/or acceptable? Each group will have its own unique way of acting and interacting with one another, much like its own culture. Finally, does each member consider themselves part of the group or what is their perception of wholeness? Each person connects to the group and the actions/decisions that occur. For example, the way you speak about your business or organization – is it "we" and "us" or is it "they" and "them" type language? Do you experience a strong reaction when someone in your group makes an inappropriate comment or does something wrong? Do you feel proud when a group member achieves something great? That strong connection to the whole unit is what causes these feelings and reactions.

Successful Teams

Now that we know what groups are in general, let us focus on implementing criteria to achieve a high level of success. Just because a group may complete a project does not mean it is the best quality. Let us examine some common characteristics of great teams.

Have Standards for Group Member Selection

Say you have the advantage of picking your own group for a project. Yes, the initial thought might be to pick people you like such as friends or colleagues. That is great and all, but are they really the best individuals to group together to make an exemplary final product? Go back to those elementary school days as you were picking teams for sports like baseball. You do not want 10 pitchers on your team, but instead

© fizkes/Shutterstock.com

you will need to choose people to cover a variety of positions. Some skills to consider include common goals, strengths/weaknesses, time management, research/writing abilities, presentation skills, technologically savvy, etc.

Clear Leadership

Make sure your team has a clear understanding of how leadership works within your group. Is one person in-charge? Is a different individual in control of each portion of the project? You want an organizational structure that makes sense for when decisions need to be made or problems arise. We will talk more about leadership styles later in this chapter.

Member Responsibilities

Once you know how leadership works within the group, be sure that each person has their own individual responsibilities. Although initially it may seem like a blessing to have nothing to do, it can be very frustrating to not contribute (or have a say) in the project. In addition, by assigning each person a task, it becomes easier to hold him/her accountable for work. There are two types of roles you may have within your group: task roles and social roles. **Task roles** relate directly to the project and the different "tasks" you are assigned to complete. Are you the speaker, note taker, tech person, researcher, etc.? The **social roles** deal with interactions among the group members and how you communicate with one another. Maybe you play the role of devil's advocate and point out what might not work. Perhaps your job is a "harmonizer" if two group members become aggressive in their communication with one another. Both types of roles exist in various forms and differ from group-to-group.

Set Goals/Objectives

Yes, you have an overarching task to complete, but how are you going to get there? Set your group up to accomplish small victories along the way to show progression in your work and meet deadlines prior to when the final project is due. Stress and frustration increase when it is the night before something needs to be submitted and one person has not completed anything, another person cannot be contacted, etc. Think of the saying, "How do you eat an elephant? One bite at a time." It is all about steadily completing work versus rushing to accomplish the entire plan in one sitting. One idea is to create a group contract together as a project begins that lays out the expectations of each group member and sets deadlines weekly/bi-weekly. (Also build in additional time for 'just in case' situations that may arise.) The contract serves as a set of guidelines that all members can refer back to if a group member is falling behind.

Stay Patient

Remember everyone has their own way of communicating, so practice those adaptive skills we discussed earlier in the book. You may have to explain your ideas a few different ways to make sure everyone in your group understands your vision. We all have different understandings, word associations, memories, etc. to sort through to make sense out of a message. It goes back to our basic communication model and field of experience. The goal is to stay calm and remember that others in the group may have to use the same approach to explain something to you. Assign a note taker at each meeting to capture ideas and document progress. If meeting virtually, record the meeting to refer back to if needed. Leaders should check in with each team member to ensure everyone is on the same page and understands their role. Group work is difficult so being patient with one another can go a long way to promote success!

Leadership in Groups

If you have ever led a group of people, whether for a class project or in the workplace, you know the high demands that come with that position. It is important to realize, just like with communicating, there is more than one way to lead correctly. It depends on the requirements of the job and the people involved. First let us examine leadership approaches discussed by mindtools.com, and then we will cover some different types of power that are involved with leadership roles.

Autocratic leader – This would be your dictator situation. The autocratic leader makes decisions on their own without necessarily consulting others in the group. Sometimes, this is necessary if you have to make a quick decision, but it can be deflating if used constantly. Why bother having a group if you are going to make all the decisions yourself?

Democratic leader – Although the democratic leader makes the final choice about how to proceed, they do turn to their team to discuss issues, brainstorm ideas, and gather information from their team to help guide their decision.

Laissez-faire leader – This person is the "hands off" leader. The group members alone decide all deadlines, decisions, etc. The leader serves as a 'go-to' for advice or suggestions, but it all goes back to how the group wants to function.

Power

Taking the role of a leader comes with a lot of demands and additional pressures.

© Anton_Ivanov/Shutterstock.com

There's a great quote from the Spider-Man series that says, "With great power comes great responsibility." This is very true for leaders in any situation. Although there are different types of powers to use, it is important to remember that your decision as a leader impacts others around you, so be sure to consider all of the consequences. Let us examine the different types of powers that exist.

Legitimate Power – a person who was elected or appointed to that position. This means that the person has power becomes it comes with the job, and it was decided they would work in that role. If your group decides to put one person in charge of monitoring the entire project, this is legitimate power. Hiring committees searching for a new supervisor would be granting legitimate power to the candidate selected for the job.

Referent Power – This is an individual that you "refer" to because you respect or admire them as an individual. They may not necessarily be your supervisor, but you trust their judgment on certain situations. Think someone in your workplace who has been there for a long time that you could turn to with questions or concerns. By seeking and taking their advice, you have given them referent power. You may ask this trusted individual if they are willing to serve as your mentor (if you organization does not assign one) just to ensure it is ok to ask them for advice as you gain experience in your new role.

Expert Power – An individual with expertise on the subject matter or task. Perhaps you were given a project that includes presenting information to a crowd of investors, and one of your group members happens to be part of Toastmasters (a public speaking organization). Well, since they have knowledge of how to prepare a presentation and give speeches frequently, they would be a great "expert" to turn to for that portion of the project. Some organizations assign a mentor to new employees to help them learn the rules and processes in the company and have someone other than the boss they can turn to with questions. This person would be considered an 'expert' because leadership trusts them to provide the new team member with accurate information.

Reward Power – This person has the ability to give perks to others when work is completed. Some organizations give bonuses, time off, vacations, etc. for meeting and/or exceeding goals for the year. If not monetary rewards, a leader can (and should) recognize good work throughout the year. Consider ideas like a monthly 'good news' email, nominations for awards like employee of the month, or even a simple thank you card. It makes your team members feel good to know that you acknowledge and appreciate their efforts.

Coercive Power – On the flip side of reward power, coercive means you have the ability to punish if tasks are not up to standards. Forcing individuals to work late or on weekends, being written up at work, pay cuts, etc. With both reward and coercive power, it is important to follow through in order for these types of power to be effective. If you make promises (either positive or negative), you better hold up your end of the deal or face losing all credibility with your team. If you promise rewards, do not deliver, and then make other promises again, why should your group believe you the second time? The same goes for negative consequences; if rules are not enforced for one individual then other team members question why they have to follow the guidelines themselves.

Pros of Group Work

So, there are reasons why working in a group can be positive. Granted these are based on the "good" group experience (we will talk about the cons of group work next). Just because one person could possibly accomplish the task does not mean it is necessarily the best product or worth all the extra effort to complete something alone. Here are some common pros of groups.

Division of Labor

Our guess is that a team/committee was formed because the project is pretty big. There may be a lot of moving parts and different details to take care of in order for everything to come together. Having more people to split up the work makes it easier so that everyone has a small job to complete versus one very overwhelmed colleague! For example, think about if your business decided to choose a new company to create and/or update your website. Every department and service(s) provided by your business is impacted by one change. It would be necessary to include at least one person from each division (or collect questions and different considerations from groups) to create a website that accurately represents all aspects of your business.

Connections and Creativity

Each person has strengths, backgrounds, and ideas that can lead to a really great final product. Think about what we discussed concerning picking your team; you do not want everyone to be exactly the same as you. Diversity is a good thing!

Think about all the different components that may be required with a large project: research, writing, presentation, aids, media, etc. One of your group members might be really great with technology, while another has no problem getting up in front of a large crowd. Why not put the best person for the job in the right position to be successful? In addition, having other people to throw out a variety of ideas can really get the creative juices flowing. Sometimes, when we work alone, we may struggle to get started or find an idea. Groups allow the opportunity to toss around lots of different ideas and approaches to determine the best method for success.

© fizkes/Shutterstock.com

Detail-Oriented

How many times have you written and edited one of your own papers and thought, "This is great work". Then your instructor gives it back to you and it is covered in red ink from all the corrections, spelling mistakes, etc. Unfortunately, when we focus on our work for an extended time, we read through information the way it is "supposed" to look versus noticing the mistakes. The good thing about group work is that more sets of eyes will look at each part of the project along the way. Each member can contribute ideas, suggestions, and correct errors throughout the process, so a solid final product is submitted. (Keep this is mind for any paper or project you have to complete individually too! Swap papers with someone at least once before you turn in your assignment to catch those tiny errors.)

Cons of Group Work

Now we are guessing many of you are thinking "yeah right, pros of group work". How many of us have had those terrible group experiences and ended up doing all of the work ourselves? Yes, there are some cons to working in small groups.

Time

© zuperia/Shutterstock.com

This is probably the biggest constraint any group faces when working on a project. Regardless of if you are in college or the workplace, each of us has obligations beyond the project including other classes, families, work, etc. The hard part is collaborating and trying to find a way to complete all the tasks. This may mean meetings after hours and/or using technology (texting, web documents, virtual meetings) to finish the work.

Conformity Pressures

Sometimes, we are lucky enough to have a choice of whom we work with on a project; other times, we are volunteered/told (aka "volun – told") you have been assigned to a group. Regardless of the situation, both types of groups can suffer from the pressure to conform and work with one another. For people who prefer to work alone, the group situation can be torture! Procrastinators will stress "Type A"—personality people. Last minute preppers will feel constantly nagged by the over-achievers to finish their portion of the project. Despite everything, each person has to find a way to work with others.

Groupthink

Go back to our earlier discussion about working with close friends or colleagues. Another reason to perhaps avoid just working with your peers is to dodge experiencing what is called groupthink. Solomon (2006) defined **groupthink** as occurring ". . . when a group of individuals aims to reach consensus on a controversial topic. Peer pressure, as well as pressure from those in authority (if present in the group), leads dissenting individuals to change their minds and, perhaps as important, not to share their knowledge of contrary evidence." (p. 31).

© holbox/Shutterstock.com

Basically, the group members stop analyzing and critiquing each other's ideas and just proceed with a suggestion even though it may not be the best option or correct. The reasons groupthink occurs vary from avoiding hurting your friend's feelings, wanting to be viewed as "agreeable" and a positive group member, or even a lack of caring about making a decision and wanting to get the project finished.

Signs to Be Aware of

All groups will face struggles and hardships while working with one another. If your team is going to work together over an extended period of time (versus a single project), there are some keys signs to recognize and hopefully prevent additional negativity. Courtney (2017) highlights five items to be aware of when working with others.

1. Working in Silos. This is a problem in larger groups and organizations – specific departments, building floors, office mates, etc. who work in and out, day-to-day with their small group of people and do not interact with others throughout the organization. Courtney (2017) notes this may cause a "not my job mentality" where if it does not directly impact that team's area then it is not their problem. Think of the saying, "not my circus, not my monkeys" in regards to silos. Unfortunately this attitude often leads to dissension and dissatisfaction within the organization. Individuals avoid contributing suggestions and ideas that may ultimately solve the problem, but instead choose to steer clear of the discussion. Silos become more of a concern if teams are completing work virtually. Many organizations use platforms like Zoom and Teams to continue working from home. Imagine how isolated a person might feel if they NEVER had the opportunity to interact with anyone except through a computer screen.

2. Blind agreement. We are hitting that groupthink con once again. The team stops critically analyzing suggestions and ideas produced. Decisions might be made and agreed upon only because the boss presented it. The team may be debating what is worse: the idea presented by the leader or speaking up against the leader's idea? Marquet (2015) asked leaders across the globe to answer (in one word) why individuals would not speak up. The number one answer was fear. Groupthink is a frequent outcome if no one is willing (or able) to question the boss. As a good leader, it is important to recognize the power that comes with your role, and employees may feel intimidated to question

or discuss decisions. One suggestion is to solicit feedback from your employees anonymously so they feel safe sharing their thoughts and opinions.

3. Exhaustion. This is described as 1) everything is urgent and needs attention immediately or 2) not saying 'no' to tasks.

It is understandable that some days you will have to stay late, put in a few extra hours, and/or work through lunch. It is unfair to ask your team to work that hard, that much, all of the time and not get tired. Multiple employees discussed the burnout experienced with the pandemic. The immediate adjustments needed in how/when/where to complete work, the increased use of technology, and feelings of never 'being off the clock' impacted the level of exhaustion felt by workers. The second type of exhaustion is very common, especially with your all-star employees. These individuals produce quality work and are go-to individuals when you need something done; however, these folks have a very hard time saying no. Recognize that boundaries need to be set and high demands cannot be maintained for long without experiencing burnout. Ask the employee, "Are you saying yes because I am asking or do you really have the time to accept this task?"

4. Stagnation. Nothing ever changes. It is the purgatory of the workplace. Team members may present new ideas, technology, programs, etc., but are consistently told no. In addition, there is no opportunity for advancement or growth within the organization. With consistent 'no's to ideas or advancement, many employees stop trying to implement positive changes (or just stop trying as a whole). Often workers will either just do their job day in/day out without truly caring or potentially leave to find an organization with more opportunities.

5. Aggression. Very much like a volcano, pressures to perform and frustration continuously build until there is an explosion that can be physical and/or emotional. Oftentimes, unfortunately, supervisors may focus only on the blowup and not what caused the reaction in the first place. Pay attention to the "word on the street" among your employees. What topics are discussed? What questions keep arising? Are workers stressed about new policies or programs? The sooner problems are addressed the more likely you can avoid the explosion.

© Mopic/Shutterstock.com

Moving Past Barriers

We know that group work can be difficult, but there are things each group (and each individual member) can do to try and move past those tricky situations. Several researchers (Bellomo, 2021; Katzenbach & Smith, 1999) discussed steps to "getting unstuck" when working with teams.

1. Revisit the basics. Sometimes a group may need to go back to the drawing board on a project. Although this may seem like a lot of work to completely start over, sometimes it is less effort to start fresh versus trying to bulldoze through a problem. A new beginning also provides for clarification of the expectations, what needs to be accomplished, and to ensure that everyone is on the same page.

2. Go for small wins. A quote from Lao Tzu fits this step perfectly. "A journey of a thousand miles begins with a single step". Yes, your group will eventually get to the end of the "journey" but that does not mean you do not hit milestones along the way. A large task can seem daunting, but breaking it into smaller goals makes a project seem more achievable, and you will have accomplishments to celebrate along the way.

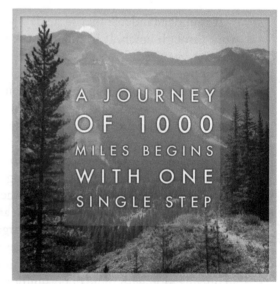

A JOURNEY OF 1000 MILES BEGINS WITH ONE SINGLE STEP

© Melissa King/Shutterstock.com

3. Maintain Performance Management and Team Engagement. Both items are especially important if working at a distance because supervisors cannot "see" their employees working, if they are struggling with a task, or making progress towards accomplishing a goal. Each time your group meets (whether

in person or online) take a moment to review upcoming deadlines, next steps in the process, and ask for progress reports. Engagement can be one-on-one or as a group, but it is an opportunity to maintain connections and relationships among the team and with the supervisor. As a boss, you want to occasionally check in with your employees just to say "hi" and see how everything is going. You do not want your only interaction to be when you have to reprimand them!

4. Inject new information and approaches. Sometimes we cannot see the forest for the trees. When a group works together for a while, you start clicking (which is a good thing), but can also lead to stagnation and frustration when problems arise. A new perspective can breathe life back into a project. Ask others, including supervisors, for their opinions about your progress and the group's goal. Outside individuals can provide different alternatives and thoughts to get the team back on track.

5. Take advantage of facilitators or training. Facilitators can be both inside and outside the organization, but can provide useful assistance to a group in need. Depending on what issue the group faces, options can include team-building exercises, communication tactics, different problem-solving techniques, etc. Some additional training may be required to possibly complete the project (such as moving to a new computer system), so it is important to have all the key players in the group ready to learn. It also serves as a bonding experience between group members.

6. Change up the roles assigned in the group, including the leader. Sometimes, a more dramatic change is needed to move forward. Shifting team members might be necessary to get "unstuck" and allows individuals to look at a problem from a different perspective. If possible, maybe switch out a group member and bring in a a new person to the team. As we know, not all groups function well together, so changing the individuals could ultimately help the entire organization; however, this might not be a viable option. Some groups/committees may have term limits that require members to serve for a certain time period, say 1-3 years, and then rotate off of the team to allow other individuals to gain experience working with that group as well.

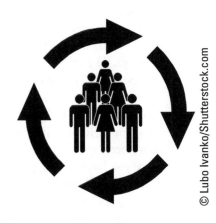

© Lubo Ivanko/Shutterstock.com

Problem-Solving Process

No matter the task at hand, there are common steps that each kind of group should perform in order to accomplish their goal. Evans and Evans (2002) discussed how John Dewey (remember the Dewey system

© iQoncept/Shutterstock.com

in your library?) introduced a reflective thinking model, which we now know as the problem-solving process today. Each of the six steps serves as a roadmap for teams to follow as they make decisions, and it also gives groups the opportunity to celebrate achievements along the way.

1. Defining the Problem. Think about your thesis statement for a speech – what is it all about? What is the issue you have to solve or the task at hand?
2. Analyze the Problem. Once you understand the overarching issue, the group then begins digging into all of the possibilities out there. What research already exists on my topic? What has been tried before? Before the group starts discussing the options together, there is one more crucial step. How are you going to make decisions? Be sure that you have a plan in place for group interactions and decision-making.
3. Suggest Possible Solutions. You have done your homework, now it is time to come together with everyone's ideas. The brainstorming phase begins! Initially, try silent brainstorming with your group. One option is to set a timer for 1 minute and each group member write down every idea they have about the project. This is the time to write down every idea (no matter how crazy or expensive) that comes into your head! An outrageous thought might be the right choice which will be examined in Step #4.
4. Developing and Comparing Solutions. Now you get to see what your teammates are thinking. The silent brainstorming approach works great compared with an open brainstorming session for several reasons. 1) Introverted and/or shy people have the opportunity to add input versus being forced to speak up. 2) There is not the awkward silence as everyone waits for somebody to speak. 3) It is hard to suggest different ideas if you are constantly shut down. For example, let us say John makes one suggestion and the group says no. Then John presents a second option but the team rejects it again. Is John going to keep speaking up? Probably not. Who knows, idea number three might have been an amazing solution, but the group misses the opportunity to hear it. Once again, make sure you have a clear plan for how you will discuss items and compare all of the different options presented. Consider items such as how much it will cost, is there enough time, and other factors that could impact the team's choice.
5. Select the Solution. You have weighed all of the options, now it is time to make a decision and start working to complete the task.
6. Implementing the Solution. The group has a clear understanding of the goal and how they are going to achieve it. Now, it is time to break up the work and assign responsibilities, deadlines, and test to make sure the choice fulfills the initial problem as it was presented in step number one.

Stages of Group Development

Finally, let us take an overarching view of different steps groups experience as a whole. The phases of the group development concept were first originated by Tuckman in 1965 and still remain a pivotal layout to describe how groups function. Frances (2008) discussed the four stages in her article.

Forming – the initial orientation. This is where groups come together and start interaction. This phase may take some time, especially, if you are unfamiliar with others on the team. At the very least, you have to learn each other's names! Plus it is important to identify what department each person represents and their connection to the task at hand.

Storming – conflict over power and authority. Now keep in mind there are two types of conflict: productive and destructive. Productive conflict is what you want to occur in the storming phase. The group is figuring out the task, which person is responsible for different aspects, etc. Destructive conflict happens when communication begins to break down and teammates focus on issues and complaints with one another versus completing the work.

Norming – the group emerges. Roles are established, tasks are assigned, and the group gets busy working. There may not be a great deal of communication taking place in this phase, as everyone knows what he or she needs to accomplish.

Performing – the reinforcement stage. Not all groups are smooth sailing (as we have discussed in our chapter), so the performing phase happens when a group faces a problem or unanticipated situation. Performing fortifies each person's responsibilities and goals for the overall project. For example, as your team is making progress, your person assigned to tech design realizes the amount of work to complete is more than the group initially estimated. For the performing stage, a good decision might be for the group to go back to the Storming phase and redistribute responsibilities to have another person help with that portion of the project.

We covered a lot in the chapter including group characteristics, pros/cons, and how to deal with stressful situations. Although you may be thinking, "why in the world would I ever work in a group?" know that the positives can outweigh the negatives in the long term. Remember that even if not assigned a specific task with a certain group of people, you are part of team in your classrooms and in the workplace. It is important to focus on the task at hand and deal with conflicts versus becoming stagnant and dissatisfied with those around you. Hopefully, we have provided some useful ideas for overcoming barriers and having a great group experience.

REFERENCES

Bellomo, T. (2021). The true test of virtual teams. *TD: Talent Development, 75*(2), 34–39.

Campion, L. L. & Campion, E. D. (2020). Leading matters: Take it from the professionals – a high-level overview of virtual leadership according to educational technology scholars (and a few others). *TechTrends, 64,* 182–184.

Courtney, C. (2017). Top 5 signs of a dysfunctional team. *Veterinary Team Brief, 5*(2), 21–25.

Evans, A. L. & Evans, V. (2002). Leadership workshop. *Education, 123*(1), 18–30.

Frances, M. (2008). Stages of group development – A PCP approach. *Personal Construct Theory & Practice, 5,* 10–18. Retrieved from: www.pcp-net.org/journal/pctp08/frances08.pdf.

Jensen, A. D. & Chilberg, J. C. (1991). *Small Group Communication. Theory and Application.* Belmont, CA: Wadsworth Publishing Company.

Katzenbach, J. R. & Smith, D. K. (1999). *The Wisdom of Teams. Creating the High-Performance Organization.* New York, NY: HarperCollins Publishers Inc.

Marquet, D. (2015). Quit the masquerade and have meetings that matter. *Leader to Leader, 2015*(78), 43–48.

Leadership styles: Choosing the right approach for the situation. (n.d.). Retrieved May 25, 2017, from https://www.mindtools.com/pages/article/newLDR_84.htm

Solomon, M. (2006). Groupthink versus the wisdom of crowds: The social epistemology of deliberation and dissent. *Southern Journal of Philosophy, 44,* 28–42.

Chapter
18 The Future

We title the final chapter of the text *The Future* because we wish to leave you with thoughts of the future and your work in business communication and beyond. The future can mean many things: self-driving cars, virtual realities and parallel worlds, average humans in space, and we are still waiting for those hover boards from Back to the Future.

For our last remarks on *Business Communication in a Technological World*, we turn our attention to two main areas. The first is a general discussion of what the future of technological communication and speech communication may look like. The second is a more specific challenge for your future as someone who will live and work inside the constructs of business and organizational communication.

The Future

In an unrelated project to this textbook, the authors conducted research inquiring about participants' attitudes on the future use of technology in the college classroom. About half of the respondents suggested that PowerPoint would remain the gold standard for making presentations in the speech situation as of this second edition in 2023, PowerPoint still remains the gold standard of presentations. The main change has been the channel, or how the PowerPoint is used. In education and business, when the pandemic struck many people simply put their old PowerPoint presentations on Zoom. Hopefully we all know now that this method does not simply transfer one-to-one. In most cases PowerPoint presentations need to be altered to match the audience and the space. The other half of the respondents thought there may be things like holograms, easier PowerPoint integration with hardware, and new software completely. So, when considering the presentation arenas and what you have studied in this course and text, what do you think the future of presentation is going to look like in professional presentations and speeches? Classrooms? Boardrooms?

This question is important because ultimately, regardless of the platform of technology used to make presentations and/or communicate in the business world and life, one thing remains the same: the fundamental principles of the communication model. There will always be a sender, receiver, message, channel, noise, feedback, and environment. In the first edition of this text we wrote: The important part is to be able to adapt to what the future may throw us. The pandemic has shown us as business communicators we needed to be nimble and adapt to what this "new future" Remember just 10 years ago, it was not really acceptable or common practice to conduct an interview via Skype. Companies would fly candidates across the country for an hour-long interview. Of course today, the opposite is true. In fact, textbooks like this one are attempting to add online interviewing skills to the cadre of tools students gain in communication courses.

Google Docs are another example of how technology and communication have converged as the future marched on. What started as a clunky platform called Google Drive has now eased into a seamless collaborative working platform. Students and professionals alike can share and edit in real-time. Again, the elements of good writing and etiquette are necessary. The technology may change as time moves on, but the basic elements of speech communication remain the same. Who knows what five years from now will look like regarding technology, many of our discussion terms here could be dated, but the need to transfer information via communication channels will remain constant.

As mentioned in previous chapters, it is not possible for PowerPoint to take over and make a speech for the presenter. Underprepared speakers who over-rely on technology still perform mediocre presentations. It is important to be mindful of this.

It is also important to be mindful of technology in general when communicating in the business and professional worlds. We often encounter colleagues and friends who say things like, "I'm not good at technology," or "I don't do technology." The truth is there is no hiding from technology. This mantra continued throughout the pandemic and still continues. Technology is cumbersome to learn in many cases and often people worry

that as soon as they learn it, it may be obsolete. When people had to adjust quickly to meet the demands of an uncertain future it was amazing how much and how fast people could learn. The interesting part was many times individuals were learning in isolation, so it was (and still is) quite interesting the various levels of knowledge self-taught technologists learned when acquiring new skills. More and more functions of the communication event have moved to technological platforms. Consider online training videos for human resource functions or online classroom opportunities in hybrid and distance learning.

The way we interface in our daily lives has changed in many ways thanks in part to smartphones and social media. UberEats and other delivery applications have changed the way we call, order, and wait for home delivery of food. Uber, in general, has changed the transportation world forever. The way we communicate with our drivers, the app, and rideshare has revolutionized the way we expect to move about freely.

The Internet of Things (IOT) is a thriving ecosystem of interconnected digital and technological communication things, not people, are communicating with each other via the Web. Imagine if your washing machine could order its own detergent or your car could get its own gas. A step toward this began with Amazon's dash buttons. These did not catch on, and you'd be pressed to find someone who used or who is using them. Instead, Amazon's Alexas and echos have replaced button pushing with simple voice commands like, "Alexa order more Tide detergent." Essentially, when you run out of laundry detergent, you can simply tell "Alexa", which then sends the request to your account and the detergent appears on your door that day or tomorrow.

We foresee more options and applications to come as people adopt and engage with this type of technology and accept communication with artificial devices.

The National Communication Association is one of the nation's largest professional organizations for members who study and work in the large disciplines housed under the communication moniker. The association is organized by division of interest: business communication, health communication, public address, and many more. One of those divisions is Communication and the Future. This division is comprised of people who study the convergence of communication theory and practices with the study of future-oriented thinking and things.

We mention this exciting division of scholars to highlight people are studying and forecasting the ways in which we may communicate in the future. Many of the literary articles from the division discuss things like virtual reality and augmented reality. Virtual being completely separate and replicable of real reality; augmented being adaptive to existing reality. Some scholars predict through phenomenology, history, and analysis that technology will continue to inform the ways in which we communicate. Whether through Alexa or virtual reality glasses, the important thing to remember is the communication model: who is the intended receiver of your communication, what is the channel, and how can you best eliminate noise?

© violetkaipa/Shutterstock.com

Your Future

The future is now in your hands! This text discussed many theories and skills for effective and professional communication in work and in life. The good news about human communication is you will always use it. You can always refine your skills and learn more ways to have your messages better received by others. We think this is exciting, we did also write a textbook about it—so others may not be as hyped about communication as we are. However, powerful communication is a tool and we challenge all of our students to continue on their journeys of being better-understood, well-presented, effective, and professional communicators. Here we offer a few ways you can do this beyond the conclusion of this course.

© Igor Bulgarin/Shutterstock.com

© Peter Hansen/Shutterstock.com

Acting Classes

This situation has happened multiple times: A student pops into the office after having taken a business communication course. He is eager and excited to keep going on the journey of becoming a master communicator. He asks what other classes he can take to improve in this arena to which we reply, "Take an acting class." Then what typically happens is a quick, "I could never do that!" And just like that this student is placing negative self-talk ahead of the desire to improve communication skills.

The bottom line: acting classes for non-majors and beginners are perfect ways to improve body movement, impromptu work, nerves, vocal quality and characteristics, memorization, interaction, and emotion. Students are exposed to a wide array of modalities to explore acting and understanding communication and movement. One may work on solo monologues, partnered scenes, character work for different types of accents and portrayal of others, and the list goes on. We cannot stress enough how much an acting class may help a student continue to grow in the world of business communication. In larger colleges and universities, there may be improvisation classes, which help you think your feet, and some programs offer improvisations for business—where students learn ways to improve their sales and professional skills. At the time of the second edition of this text, digital storytelling and data analytics have become popular courses for programs across the country. Different in nature, the idea of analyzing data and then creating the message about it seem to fit together nicely. Perhaps you are an analytics student who needs the nudge into the digital storytelling world. Go for it!

Avoiding Bad Habits

We encourage you, no we BEG of you, to not forget the principles in this text when you are exposed to mediocre forms of professional communication in your other classes and at work. Please strive to be the best PowerPoint presenter in your other classes and professionally. As much as reading slides out loud to audiences passes for mediocre presenting in other courses, please remember to move beyond this. Please strive to be a professional communicator with your faculty, peers, employees, and management teams. Remember to write well and send thank-you notes. Remember to dress well and do your best to have your message understood. Do your best to speak well and be memorable.

Another bad habit we find our students engage in is not speaking up in other classes, even on Zoom! There is no doubt online meetings can be awkward between talking over each other and/or technology issues. Yet, speaking up more frequently can ease the unease of speaking in public online situations.. Some students open up in our classrooms because they feel comfortable and safe, yet sometimes they confess that in their other classes they never speak up. Change this! Answer those questions. Lead a group. Get to know the professor. Communicate with peers for notes and beyond. It may sound like a small thing, but little acts like this daily will immensely improve your communication skills.

Read

With hundreds of television programs available across all media devices and platforms, it is quite easy to forget about the pastime of reading. The truth is, though, reading is not just a "pastime." Even reading books for pleasure is a form of education. When we read, we subtly learn writing conventions, styles, and techniques. The more you read, the more you are exposed to these conventions. Even reading fiction novels can help improve your writing skills. Improved writing skills have the possibility to improve formal speaking and professional communication as well.

Another aspect of reading for improved professional communication is to read popular trade books on professional speaking. One example is *TED Talks* by Chris Anderson, the head of TED. This popular easy read breaks down the characteristics of what makes a good TEDTalk and how the reader can capitalize on these skills. Many people already watch and enjoy Ted Talks—why do people not employ the Ted techniques themselves? They can! This book highlights those principles. There are many books similar to this one on the market and it is best to read the Amazon reviews and pick the one best for your time and desires.

© aslysun/Shutterstock.com

Listen

Much like reading, another way to improve speaking and professional skills is to listen and watch exemplary speeches. We just mentioned TED Talks and this is one of the best places to start. TED also has an app you can download to take podcasts of TED Talks with you on the go. YouTube is another avenue for discovering excellent presentations. Throughout this journey, you will also see presentations you do not like. This is okay. Understand what is not good speaking and what further steps are needed toward doing the effective speaking you want to create.

© pathdoc/Shutterstock.com

Volunteer

Another avenue to improving professional communication skills is in a low-stakes environment like volunteering or joining a club. Many organizations are happy just to have quality volunteers or members who do a nice job. What a wonderful outlet this could be for you to step up and speak out. If you make a speaking mistake, no one will fire you or criticize you. With volunteering, showing up and participating is most of the battle. People would not care that you are also secretly practicing your communication skills—they will embrace you. The same is true for school and civic clubs and groups. Members are always seeking more members to carry on with the group. This is an excellent place for you to practice professional communication and leadership skills.

© Rawpixel.com/Shutterstock.com

Summary

It is our sincere hope you enjoyed your journey through *Business Communication in a Technological World.* We attempted to structure the book using traditional and important communication concepts and theories to support progressive and professional forms of business communication. Social media and technology are here to stay, and learning to effectively communicate using those tools in various contexts is the key to being a successful professional.

We began our text with the basic understanding of the communication model, and we end with an optimistic look to the future that includes our students effectively engaging in more ways to improve their skills. We hope the concepts and chapters of this text capitalize on the talents you already have and possibly add a few new ones to the toolbox. Good luck!

© Gustavo Frazao/Shutterstock.com

Summary